FIELD HOUSE

Population and the Environment

Population and the Environment

The Linacre Lectures 1993–4

Edited by

BRYAN CARTLEDGE

Principal of Linacre College
University of Oxford

Oxford   New York   Tokyo
OXFORD UNIVERSITY PRESS
1995

Oxford University Press, Walton Street, Oxford OX2 6DP

Oxford   New York
Athens   Auckland   Bangkok   Bombay
Calcutta   Cape Town   Dar es Salaam   Delhi
Florence   Hong Kong   Istanbul   Karachi
Kuala Lumpur   Madras   Madrid   Melbourne
Mexico City   Nairobi   Paris   Singapore
Taipei   Tokyo   Toronto
and associated companies in
Berlin   Ibadan

Oxford is a trade mark of Oxford University Press

Published in the United States
by Oxford University Press Inc., New York

© Oxford University Press, 1995

A catalogue record for this book is available from the British Library

Library of Congress Cataloging in Publication Data
(Data available)

ISBN 0 19 854842 7 (Hbk)
ISBN 0 19 854 841 9   (Pbk)

Typeset by Colset Private Limited, Singapore
Printed in Great Britain by
Biddles Ltd, Guildford and Kings Lynn

Acknowledgements

This fourth series of Linacre Lectures is the first to be sponsored by British Petroleum plc. I am happy to record the gratitude of Linacre College, and of Oxford University, to BP for making the continuation of the Lectures possible; this gratitude is, I know, shared by all those who attend the Lectures and the even larger number worldwide who read them subsequently in this published form. This is yet another demonstration of the serious concern for environmental issues for which BP is well-known.

Once again, I am most grateful to Frances Morphy for devoting her time and her expertise to the task of preparing our contributors' texts for submission to the Oxford University Press; to Jane Edwards, our College Secretary, for her hard work and enthusiasm in co-ordinating the arrangements of the Lectures themselves; and, of course, to our Lecturers for supporting Linacre's project and for maintaining the distinction which it has acquired.

Linacre College, Oxford   B.G.C.
August 1994

Contents

Authors

Sir Bryan Cartledge
Principal, Linacre College, Oxford

Professor John Clarke, DL
Emeritus Professor of Geography, University of Durham

Dr Murray Feshbach
Research Professor of Demography, Georgetown University, Washington DC, USA

The Right Reverend Richard Harries
Bishop of Oxford

Professor Geoffrey Ainsworth Harrison
Professor of Biological Anthropology, University of Oxford (retired)

Professor R. B. Heap, FRS
Director BBSRS Institute of Animal Physiology and Genetics Research at Babraham, Cambridge

The Right Reverend John Jukes OFM (Conv)
Roman Catholic Bishop of Strathearn

Professor Martin Parry
Professor of Environmental Management and Director of Environmental Studies, University College, London

Dr Pramilla Senanayake
Assistant Secretary-General, International Planned Parenthood Federation

Introduction
Bryan Cartledge

The problem is simply stated. By the end of the twenty-first century — and possibly within the lifetime of some of today's infants and toddlers — the population of our planet is likely to have doubled, as it has done during the past fifty years. Brian Heap (below, page 48) takes the relatively optimistic view that the world's population will reach a plateau of about 10 billion by 2100. A contributor to the last series of Linacre Lectures (John Seaman in *Health and the Environment*, OUP 1994), on the basis of forecasts by the UN Population Fund, predicted a figure of 11 billion by the year 2060. In this series, Geoffrey Harrison cites the illustrative estimate that if recent growth rates were to continue for a thousand years there would be 1700 people to each square yard of the Earth's surface, land and sea: extrapolation is not predictive but it does help to concentrate the mind.

John Clarke points out that global or national population figures can be misleading and lead to over-simplifications of the population/environment relationship; but his more differentiated approach underlines rather than mitigates the problem. In a hundred years' time the 10 billion (for the sake of argument) members of the human race will not, obviously, be distributed evenly over the earth's land surface: they will be overwhelmingly concentrated in economic core areas, in sprawling mega-cities not far from coasts. Leaving aside, for the moment, the Earth's capacity to sustain this number of people — its so-called 'carrying capacity' — the purely social implications of this scenario are hair-raising, as any recent visitor to Mexico City, Cairo, or Beijing will readily confirm. In the short term it is desirable, in the medium term necessary, and in the long term (Geoffrey Harrison's thousand years) clearly essential to slow and if possible to halt world population growth on a sustainable plateau. Between them the contributors to this volume identify most of the factors which militate both for and against the achievement of this objective.

Contraceptive technology, as Geoffrey Harrison points out, is by no means the whole answer to the problem: 'even if the perfect contraceptive were always to hand at no cost to every individual, fertility might well be excessive'. Most couples want to have children. In developing countries, most couples want to have as many children as possible — to maximize their chances of producing boys, to increase the family income, and to provide old-age insurance for the parents. To women without education the virtues of contraception are by no means self-evident, although — as Pramilla Senanayake stresses — it is they who have to bear the greatly enhanced risks of disease and mortality which repeated pregnancies in a degraded environment carry with them. The custom of marriage in the early teens, prevalent in many developing countries, extends female reproductive life and also debars women from the education which would reveal to them the improved quality of life which family planning can offer. The opposition of the Roman Catholic Church to contraception, reaffirmed in the encyclical *Veritatis Splendor* by the Pope and in this volume by Bishop John Jukes, has as great an impact on the public policies of governments as on the private behaviour of individual Catholics — perhaps a greater one, as Dr Senanayake implies. The unyielding position of the Church inhibits the introduction of national family planning programmes, and the provision of financial support for international programmes, in a number of countries — including many of those which need such programmes most. Finally, it must be borne in mind that the very success of the war against disease, malnutrition, puerperal and infant mortality, and pollution removes a significant constraint on population growth. The humanitarian and — in the context of economic development — practical arguments in favour of prosecuting this war to the limits of our energies and resources are, of course, overwhelming; but we have to remember that victories on one front require redoubled efforts to avoid defeat on the other.

So much for some of the negative factors in the population equation: are there countervailing factors to balance them? Our lecturers identified several. Despite all the obstacles, of human nature and of human cultures, the use of modern contraceptives has increased quite dramatically — from less than 10 per cent in the 1960s to over 50 per cent in 1992 (Senanayake). Partly as a consequence of this, the average number of children per woman in the developing countries has declined from over 6 in the late 1960s to 3.9 in the late 1980s — although in Roman Catholic Rwanda, for example, it is still 8, one of the highest fertility rates in the world. These developments have been assisted by the evolution, through tolerance to positive approval, of attitudes towards contraception in all the major religious faiths except Roman Catholic Christianity; Bishop Richard Harries, for example, gives an encouraging account of this evolution in the Anglican Church. Genetically engineered vaccines for reversible immunocontraception could eventually be a powerful ally for the family planners, although there are formidable financial and cultural obstacles to be overcome (Brian Heap). In a different context, just as the fight to improve the human environment can weaken constraints on population growth, so environmental neglect and degradation can strengthen them: atmospheric and water pollution in the former Soviet Union, for example, combined with the near-collapse of public health services, have helped both to reduce life expectancy—now down to 59 years for Russian men—and to increase infant mortality, giving Russia a negative birth rate for the first time this century (Feshbach). This is not, however, the kind of curb on population growth which one would wish to see replicated.

It emerges clearly from several of these lectures that the essential concomitants to simple contraception are education—particularly of women—and economic development; both, obviously, are in any case highly desirable in their own right. In countries where no women are enrolled in secondary education, the average woman has seven children, but where 40 per cent of all women have had a secondary education the average drops to three children (Senanayake). This is a dramatic and revealing statistic. It may owe something, however, to the higher level of economic development which is itself a precondition of rising educational enrolment. The implications of economic development for population trends are not straightforward (as Geoffrey Harrison points out). Some of the consequences of economic improvement—better nutrition, less disease, less manual labour for women—should result in greater fertility and a rising birthrate, although others—including lower infant mortality and improved social welfare provision for the old—should work in the opposite direction. Above the poverty line, rising incomes and rising expectations create the possibility of choice: material possessions and an improved quality of life compete with the unborn child for a couple's resources. Once there is money to spend on them, children become in themselves a more expensive proposition. Considerations of status and, in the mushrooming urban conglomerations, of physical space argue in favour of family planning.

Current predictions of world population trends are largely based on the view that the factors favouring restraint and family planning will ultimately prevail over the factors which militate against them—but not yet; hence the expectation of a flattening-out in 60–100 years' time at a level of about 10 billion. The nightmare scenario of human beings stacked up like battery hens is unlikely to be realized. The second major question addressed by the contributors to this volume, however, is that of whether our planet can sustain the 100 per cent increase which seems certain to occur.

The world's food supply is the most obvious area for assessment. A Linacre lecturer in an earlier series (John Seaman, already cited above) calculated that since world production of food grains alone is currently 2 billion tons annually and that since four people can reasonably subsist on a ton for a year, the current food supply should be sufficient for 8 billion people—if we stop feeding grain to cattle and converting it into alcohol. In this series, Brian Heap agrees that every continent except Africa is increasing food production faster than their populations are growing; but points out not only that Africa is a critical exception, where existing agricultural strategies cannot cope with the food gap, but also that in the developing countries as a whole subclinical malnutrition is already a permanent condition. Martin Parry shows that all the main predictive scenarios for global climatic change indicate that their effect on food production will be significantly more adverse in lower latitudes (the developing world) than in higher. In seventy-five years' time, 640 million people could be at risk from hunger, a figure which would be much higher if economic growth—particularly in the developing countries—slows down, but much lower if population growth is low and if agricultural trade is fully liberalized. One variable which does not enter directly into Martin Parry's highly sophisticated calculations but which should be borne in mind is the contribution which genetic engineering can make to arable farming and to animal husbandry: '... genetic engineering techniques ... offer the potential to increase the quantity, quality, and safety of food supplies often by overcoming geographical and climatic obstacles, by the rapid dissemination of disease resistance, and by the widespread distribution of superior genetic qualities compatible with sustainable practices' (Heap, p. 67 below). Before that potential can be realized, there are genuine apprehensions and less rational fears to be overcome in the public mind: but biotechnology could hold the key to releasing the human race from the Malthusian trap—arithmetic growth in food supply trailing behind geometric population growth—through the voluntary inhibition of human fertility accompanied by the dramatic enhancement of agricultural production. This scientific double for the twenty-first century is within our grasp so long as the development of essential legal safeguards and public education can keep pace with developments in the laboratory.

Despite the adverse impact of climatic change (resulting primarily from increased concentrations of CO_2 and other gases in the atmosphere) and of the environmental degradation which has hitherto been the inevitable concomitant of economic growth, the chances that our planet will be able to provide sufficient food for 10 billion people in one hundred years' time are reasonably good.

But 'global carrying capacity' cannot, surely, be defined solely in terms of food supply. A dramatic growth in the world's population — and an increase of 100 per cent over the next 75–100 years would certainly qualify as dramatic — has implications which are wider than a simple increase in the demand for food and water.

Over 90 per cent of the anticipated global population increase is expected to occur in the poorest regions of the developing world. It is in these same regions that internal migration from countryside to city, driven by the degradation of the rural environment — deforestation, desertification, and the depletion of fresh water supplies — is most marked. In an article which rightly attracted wide attention (*Atlantic Monthly*, February 1994) Robert Kaplan gave a vivid description of the extent to which, in three West African countries — Ivory Coast, Guinea, and Sierra Leone — the countryside is already draining into a coastal strip of dense urban slums and shanty-towns. In other regions already afflicted by desperate and endemic poverty, internal migration could be triggered by climatic change: even a small rise in sea levels, for example, could threaten millions in the delta area of Bangladesh. This process creates problems both of public health and of public order more acute than anything with which politicians and administrators have as yet had to contend; in the regions worst affected, political and administrative talent is often in short supply. Against a background of social breakdown, local conflicts arising from competition for scarce resources — especially water — could quickly become regional. Although our planet may be able to feed 10 billion people, the challenge of absorbing the pressures which they will exert on social and political structures could prove even more formidable.

Fortunately, we have enough time in which to prepare to meet the challenge; the value of doomsday scenarios is that they heighten awareness. The threat of an environmentally driven collapse of the world's social fabric may soon be sufficiently vivid to stimulate the elevation of the innate human instinct to co-operate from the level of groups to national and regional levels (Harrison, p. 45). This could, among other things, vindicate one of the more optimistic assumptions in Martin Parry's contribution, namely that the complete liberalization of agricultural trade can be achieved globally by the year 2020. As this Introduction is written (in August 1994), final preparations are under way for the United Nations Conference on Population in Cairo. To be accounted a success, the Conference will have to address not only the more obvious dimensions of the global population problem — birth control and food supply — but also the less easily quantifiable questions of social organization and political management which it poses.

1
Population and the environment: complex interrelationships
John Clarke

Professor John Clarke DL is Emeritus Professor of Geography at the University of Durham. He took his first degree and was awarded his doctorate at the University of Aberdeen, where he was appointed an Assistant Lecturer in geography in 1954. He moved to Durham a year later to take up the lectureship which he held there until 1963. He then spent 2 years in West Africa, as Professor of Geography at the University College of Sierra Leone, before returning to Durham as Reader and, from 1968, Professor of Geography — a post that he held for 22 years. Professor Clarke served as Pro-Vice-Chancellor and Sub-Warden of the university from 1984 until his retirement in 1990, when he became a Deputy Lieutenant of County Durham. He is a vice-president of the Royal Geographical Society, Chairman of the Population and Environment Committee of the International Union for the Scientific Study of Population (IUSSP), a former chairman of the International Geographical Union's (IGU) Commission on Population Geography, and the author and editor of many books on population geography, especially with reference to the developing countries. Professor Clarke is also Chairman of the North Durham Health Authority.

INTRODUCTION

The concern of this book and the series of lectures from which it derives is primarily with one of the great issues of our time, the impact of population growth upon environment, and the problems that we are posing for ourselves. It is, however, important to recognize that the interrelationships between population and environment are two way, that they vary greatly over time and space, and that they are modified by a number of intervening factors, such as the level and type of economic activities and technological development, cultural systems, social welfare, political units, and political decision-making. Too often the relationship between population growth and environmental change has been portrayed over-simplistically as a one-way process. There is a complex web of direct and indirect interactions between diverse populations and environments at local level which have varied aggregative effects at global level.

TERMINOLOGY AND DEFINITIONS

Much of the extensive literature about the interaction of population and environment is unsatisfactory, not only because the interrelationships have been over-simplified and over-generalized, but also because authors have rarely defined what they mean by 'population' and 'environment'. Both terms have been used very loosely in the popular literature, and often in a pejorative or incomplete sense; thus 'population' has been regarded simply in terms of numbers and growth, invariably being a problem which is alliteratively convenient but not always true, and 'environment' has usually been regarded as degraded or threatened by humanity, emphasizing only our negative impact upon nature. For some, population has become a bad and environment a good — perhaps a necessary viewpoint given our sometimes lamentable history of environmental stewardship. Nevertheless, too often both terms remain unspecified geographically or temporally, yet they may apply to a range of units from a small locality to the globe itself in the past, present, or future.

Population

The term 'population' is conceptually varied. Generally it means the aggregate of people residing within an administrative or geographic area. This area concept is an example of the ecological fallacy whereby the population is defined by its territory rather than by its demographic or social distinctiveness; indeed, human divisions may have been a reason for not taking a census in some parts of the world (e.g. Lebanon, Ethiopia). The areal concept arises from the origins of demography in political arithmetic and the collection of data on a country basis; but states (and their administrative subdivisions) vary hugely in areal and population size, from less than $2 \, km^2$ and 10 000 inhabitants to nearly 10 million km^2 and 1.2 billion inhabitants, and with a markedly skewed frequency distribution (Tables 1.1 and 1.2). The concept makes more geographical sense for readily identifiable areas such as the globe, continents, and islands than for many countries and administrative units which have little environmental identity or uniformity (Clarke 1976).

Table 1.1 Population sizes of countries by continent, 1991

Continent	Population in millions					
	More than 1000	100–1000	10–100	1–10	Less than 1	Total
Africa	–	–	16	28	8	52
Americas	–	2	9	15	19	45
Asia	1	5	18	18	6	48
Europe	–	1	14	15	10	40
Oceania	–	–	1	2	12	15
Total	1	8	59	77	55	200

Table 1.2 Areal sizes of countries by continent, 1991

Continent	Area in thousand km^2					
	More than 10 000	1000– 10 000	100– 1000	10–100	Less than 10	Total
Africa	–	12	23	12	5	52
Americas	–	8	11	9	17	45
Asia	–	7	22	12	7	48
Europe	1	–	18	13	8	40
Oceania	–	1	2	4	8	15
Total	1	28	76	50	45	200

States have evolved as political spaces rather than as environmental regions, and environmental patterns generally bear little relationship to political patterns. Some large countries, such as the USA and China, incorporate huge varieties of environmental zones; other small countries, such as Macau and the Maldives, fall entirely within one zone. Moreover, population data are difficult to relate to environments unless they are geocoded, and only a few countries, such as UK, Canada, USA, and France, have generated detailed geocoded population data (Clarke and Rhind 1992). Consequently, there have been remarkably few attempts to relate population numbers to altitude, latitude, climatic zones, and distance from the sea, although there is great potential for the use of geographical information systems (GIS).

There are two further complications. First, there is a tendency towards a negative exponential relationship between the size of areal units and population density, so that territorial areas such as administrative districts tend to decrease in size at a decreasing rate with increasing population density. Secondly, migration rates are higher for smaller areal units than larger ones, because most migration is over short distances and contained within large areal units. Consequently, the significance of migration in overall population change varies according to the size of the areal unit. At global level, all migration is internal and all population change is natural (being the balance of births and deaths); at ward or parish level, the balance of inward and outward migration is the main element in population change. Moreover, the relative significance of natural change and migration also has a great effect upon aspects of population structure, like age, sex, and ethnic composition.

The term 'population' is also used for more distinctive sectoral or sub-populations (e.g. female, Black, school, or Welsh-speaking populations), none of which is locationally discrete within bounded spaces; and it is also used for any group under study, such as the employees of a company or patients in a hospital.

The world's population is therefore hierarchically made up of a large number of populations classified areally, sectorally, or socially, which may vary greatly in size, structure and composition, distribution and density, and dynamics (fertility, mortality, and migration); smaller populations deviating markedly from the demographic means of larger populations. There is a danger in talking about populations as if they are just numbers rather than groups of peoples, who have never been so demographically, socially, economically, or even politically diverse. Variations in the roles of women around the world — their age of marriage, number of children, literacy, levels of education, workforce participation, political representation, etc. — admirably exemplify this diversity. It is easier to make generalizations about macro-populations (e.g. demographic transition in more or less developed countries) than about diverse micro-populations with their fluctuating rates, because of the infrequency of vital rates (1–2 per cent per annum), their irregular population structures, and the greater effect of external migration.

Explanations of demographic phenomena are also greatly affected by the level of analysis. The explanations at global level are not the same as at local level. For example, any explanation of world population distribution involves latitude, altitude, climate, and distance from the sea as principal factors; not so at all in examining population distribution within Oxfordshire. Similarly, the explanations of global fertility, mortality, and migrations differ from those at the level of the family or household. Hence there is a tendency to distinguish between micro and macro in demography, although there is no simple dichotomy with a well-defined threshold

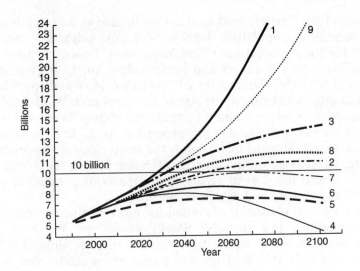

Fig. 1.1 Total projected world population 1990–2100 according to scenario. Scenario 1: constant rates; constant 1985–1990 fertility and mortality rates. Scenario 2: UN medium variant; strong fertility and mortality decline until 2025, then constant. Scenario 3: slow fertility decline; UN fertility decline 25 years delayed, UN medium mortality. Scenario 4: rapid fertility decline; TFR = 1.4 all over the world in 2025, UN medium mortality. Scenario 5: immediate replacement fertility; assumed TFR = 2.1 in 1990, UN medium mortality. Scenario 6: constant mortality; TFR = 2.1 all over the world in 2025, constant mortality. Scenario 7: slow mortality decline; UN mortality decline 25 years delayed, TFR = 2.1 in 2025. Scenario 8: rapid mortality decline; life expectancy of 80/85 years and TFR = 2.1 in 2025. Scenario 9: Third World crisis; constant fertility and 10 per cent increase in mortality in Africa and southern Asia, TFR = 2.1 in 2025 and UN mortality for the rest of the world. Note: TFR is the total fertility rate (= average number of children per woman). (After Lutz 1991.)

(Goldscheider 1971). Instead, there is a spectrum of levels from the individual to the global, sufficient to encourage care in extrapolating from the local to the national and global, or vice versa.

One other point worthy of mention is that constants play a much smaller part in population analysis than in environmental analysis, and it is the volatility and susceptibility of populations to trends, fluctuations, and shifts that make it so difficult to predict their future, especially in the long term. A glance at the contrasting possible scenarios of the total projected world population 1990–2100 illustrates this (Fig. 1.1). Hence the desire among many to try to control this unruly variability by population control.

Environment

If population is a rather ambiguous aggregative term, environment is even more so. Ignoring the more specific connotations of the term, such as those in computing, architecture, theatre, and the visual arts, three broad definitions concern us here: physical/natural, geographical, and ecological.

First is the physical/natural environment, the complex characteristics of landscapes (their climates, geology, soils, drainage, etc.) which have not been markedly changed by human impact. In fact the pervasiveness of human impact means that such landscapes are becoming ever more rare. Consequently, we tend to talk more about the geographical environment, which includes the physical environment along with our human modifications. It may therefore be subdivided in a variety of ways: inhabited/uninhabited, built/ unbuilt, urban/rural. Physical environments are not inert, but geographical environments change much more rapidly because of human action. Both change in the short and long terms through trends, fluctuations, and shifts, which are not easily distinguished because of the limitations in available data over long periods. Anthropogenic forces are also increasingly impacting upon natural phenomena in innumerable ways: animal and plant dispersal, domestication, and conservation; loss of biodiversity; deforestation; desertification; extension of scrub and grasslands; soil erosion and fertility; water flow, quantity, and quality; pollution of air, water, and land; quarrying and mining; coastal erosion and deposition; waste disposal; and so on. The impact has often been drastic, leading to rapid environmental degradation, but not all forces have been so negative, and in any case degradation is another term that is difficult to define.

One of the great scientific dilemmas of our time is to determine the relative significance of natural and human factors upon environmental changes, especially as similar physical results can occur from different physical and human processes—this has been termed the principle of equifinality (Goudie 1984). It is all the more difficult when one is considering future environmental changes, such as global warming, for a wide variety of reasons: the complexity of natural systems; their non-linear response to change; the imperfection of our models and knowledge of mechanisms; as well as the possibility of unforeseen and extreme events (Goudie 1993). Generally, it is easier to make predictions about future environmental changes than to be certain about them. Therefore, it would be wrong to assume that demographic uncertainties greatly outweigh environmental uncertainties, but probably we are more likely to be able to influence them.

The third connotation of the term 'environment' that concerns us here is ecological, defined as the external conditions or surroundings in which plants or animals live, tending to influence their development or behaviour—the environment exists because it is inhabited by organisms. The concept of the ecological environment has been popularized by its association with the growing concern that large parts of the physical environment have been misused, altered, and over-exploited to their long-term detriment or degradation (although this latter term is usually ill-defined), so that environmental conservation has become a vital issue for those concerned about our sustainable future. The concept is also associated with the concept of the ecosystem, which is the system formed by the interaction of all living organisms with the physical and chemical factors in their environment. Like populations, the boundaries of ecosystems are hard to delineate, and it is easier to deal with the Earth's ecosystem than to isolate self-contained and geographically restricted ecosystems. Perhaps this is one reason why, despite environmental changes at every level, some of which are exclusively local (e.g. change in a river channel, a road, or a cliff line), we are focusing our scientific attention and public concern upon global environmental change (GEC)—upon the greenhouse effect, stratospheric ozone depletion, acid aerosols, loss of biodiversity, land degradation, decline in water quantity and quality, and increasing urban concentration, especially in mega-cities—despite the fact that global changes have diverse local origins. The effects of human-induced climatic changes have given particular concern, and are best analysed globally, localized patterns often being too difficult to analyse outwith their broader context.

Just as there are advantages in viewing populations holistically, so the ecosystem concept has shown the advantages of this approach to the environment, which was so often previously viewed in terms of different environmental variables and from distinct disciplinary stances. On the other hand, it is imperative to remember that GEC is the aggregative result of numerous and widespread physical and human processes, which have produced a multitude of different environments, ranging from polar ice-caps to tropical rainforests, from mountain peaks to deltaic swamps, from mega-cities to dune deserts, from taiga to insular atolls.

The word 'environment' has thus evolved from a purely physical concept to one which is about complex biological interrelationships with nature, and it has expanded particularly with the growing recognition of the significance of human influence upon major environmental processes.

Environmentalism

The term 'environmentalism' has also changed in connotation. It was for long a synonym for environmental determinism, the school of thought that peoples and cultures are influenced and moulded by the physical environment, notably climate. Determinism can be traced back to Hippocrates in the fifth century BC and it has deep medieval roots, but probably attained its apogee in the nineteenth century with the works of Friedrich Ratzel. It has lived on into the twentieth century in the work of Ellen Churchill Semple, Ellsworth Huntington, and others, including the 'scientific determinism' of Griffith Taylor.

Environmental determinism reflected the powerful impress that the physical environment had upon populations in the past, affecting their distribution, density, migration, morbidity, mortality, and fertility over the long and short terms. The influence was stronger in pre-industrial times than now, when populations derived their living from primary occupations (hunting, collecting, farming, fishing, pastoralism) which were greatly affected by environmental conditions (Clarke 1972). The physical environment imposed itself particularly in determining the non-ecumene, the largely uninhabited world which is usually too cold, too dry, too high, and too rugged for human habitation. In addition, remoteness from the sea is generally a deterrent. The physical environment has also greatly influenced the patterns of population density through types of agriculture, as well as varied types of migratory movement (e.g. nomadism, transhumance, periodic migration, circulation). Environmental diseases, such as malaria, sleeping sickness, yellow fever, and river blindness, have long played a major role in morbidity and mortality patterns, and although their overall influence, and those of infectious diseases, are much reduced in more-developed countries (MDCs) they are still very important in less-developed countries (LDCs). The effect of the environment upon human fertility is much more tenuous except in areas of extremes, as at high altitudes, where reproductivity is affected.

As 'development' progressed during this century, so the crudity of the earlier deterministic concept of environmentalism was attacked and replaced by a series of other theories: the possibilism of the great French school of geographers led by Vidal de la Blache, which emphasized that human–nature relationships also result from differences in cultures which create many possibilities for using nature; the probabilism of Oscar Spate, which stresses that in any given situation there is a balance of probability; the rise of behaviouralism that explains population–environment relationships primarily through cognitive processes that underlie human behaviour, stating that people make decisions about their environments in the light of their perceptions, which are greatly influenced by cultural backgrounds; and radical/structural approaches, focusing upon structural explanations of our society and world economy in which themes of inequality, human welfare, and relevance have been prevalent.

The current connotation of environmentalism reflects these changing views, for today there is an ecocentric concern about how humanity is altering its environment and a desire to maintain ecological balance. Engendered especially by growing awareness particularly of the phenomena of global environmental changes and the variety of processes and forces that are causing them, environmentalism has moved from being a scientific theory to being a popular movement, influenced by individual and local frustration and impotence about global forces which seem to be beyond control. Some of the environmental changes, such as global warming, ozone depletion, and acid rain are still surrounded by scientific uncertainties and controversy, and predictions about their future impacts are almost inevitably speculative, especially given the possibility of future discontinuities. Environmentalism, however, is more concerned with underlying causes than with particular predictions, no matter how significant or symbolic they may be, on the wise assumption that it is better to be safe than sorry.

UNDERLYING CHANGES, 1800–2000

The changed connotation of environmentalism from the impact of environment upon humanity to the impact of humanity upon environment symbolizes the manifold changes in the world over the past two centuries since Thomas Malthus wrote *An essay on the principle of population* (1798) — changes which he could not have foreseen and which have interposed between populations and environments, transforming their interrelationships. The unsatisfactory and variously defined word 'development' is usually used to encompass the changes, so that many consider that it should be incorporated within all population–environment analyses to form a triad or troika (Wahren 1991): population–development–environment (Lutz 1994). But no single word such as development could encompass the numerous changes that have affected population–

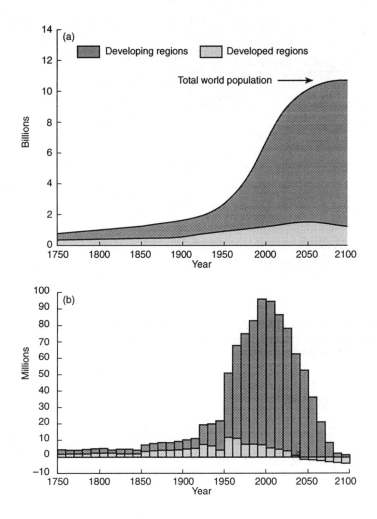

Fig. 1.2 (a) World population growth 1750–2100. (b) Average annual increase in numbers per decade, 1750–2100. (Source: Population Reference Bureau estimates, 1990.)

environment interrelationships since 1800, when the world population was only about 1 billion, with about 86 per cent living in Eurasia, especially in the three concentrations of India, China, and Europe. Although the continental distribution of population was much more uneven than now, local distribution was generally more even as there were few urban centres, only about 3 per cent of people lived in towns, the overwhelming majority living from the land.

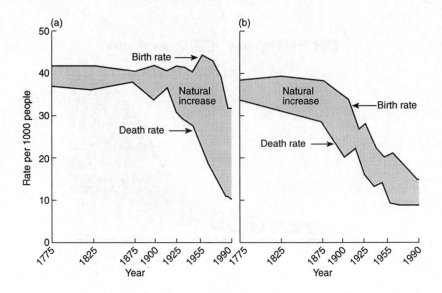

Fig. 1.3 Population growth through natural increase, 1775–1990. (a) Less-developed countries; (b) more-developed countries. (Source: Population Reference Bureau.)

Population changes

The sixfold increase of population during the years 1800–2000 (Figs 1.2 and 1.3) was achieved by differential demographic transition from high to low fertility and mortality, initially slowly in the MDCs of Europe and 'Europes overseas' over a century and a half, and more recently and more rapidly in the LDCs where, since mid-century, progress in fertility and mortality decline has been much more varied. Some of the variation can be seen in Fig. 1.4 which depicts the convergence of birth and death rates among high-income countries and the divergence among middle-income and low-income countries. Recently it has ranged from an extremely rapid transition in countries like China, South Korea, Taiwan, Hong Kong, Singapore, Thailand, Mauritius, Chile, Cuba, and Puerto Rico to a much more limited transition in many of the least-developed countries of sub-Saharan Africa and parts of Asia (e.g. Afghanistan, Nepal, Yemen), with other LDCs achieving more mortality decline than fertility decline, especially in many Muslim countries (Tabah 1992). In fact there has been great world-wide variation in fertility decline (Fig. 1.4), influenced by factors such as government policies, economic changes, female literacy, culture, and religion. Differential

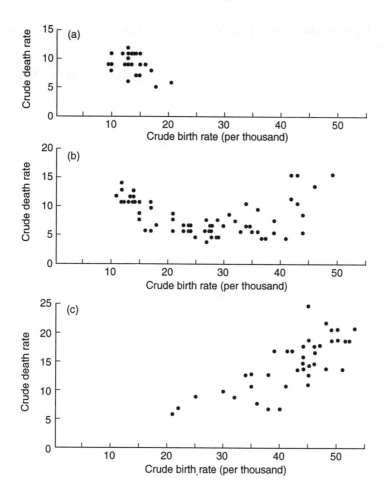

Fig. 1.4 Birth and death rates, (a) high-income countries; (b) middle-income countries; (c) low-income countries.

demographic transition has been accompanied by differential socio-demographic changes such as ageing, the spread of the nuclear family, and the rising status of women, so that there are major contrasts in these phenomena around the world today.

Just as significant from a population–environment viewpoint has been the massive redistribution of population since 1800. This took place initially through the settlement by Europeans of the less populated parts of the world: the Americas, Oceania, parts of Africa and Central Asia. Although the continental migrations involved only tens of millions and the settlements were largely peripheral, they had often devastating impacts upon the thousands of indigenous peoples

Table 1.3 Percentage world population distribution by continental region, 1800–2000

	1800	1850	1900	1950	2000 est.
Asia	64.7	65.3	54.6	54.6	59.2
Europe and former USSR	21.0	23.0	26.9	22.8	13.1
Africa	10.9	6.7	9.0	8.9	13.9
North America	0.7	2.2	5.2	6.6	4.7
Latin America	2.5	2.7	4.0	6.6	8.6
Oceania	0.2	0.2	0.4	0.5	0.5

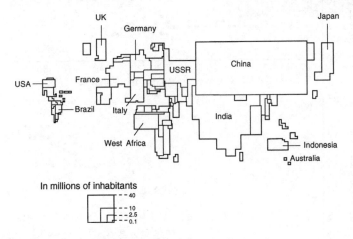

Fig. 1.5 Distribution of population by countries in 1880 (after Noin 1991).

(e.g. Tasmanians, American Indians, Caribs) and upon the colonized environments; soil erosion in New Zealand and the American Great Plains, for example, provide ample evidence that large populations are not a prerequisite for environmental degradation on a massive scale. Newcomers rarely possess the necessary knowledge of their adopted environments to care for them adequately, perceiving them and utilizing them according to their cultural traditions. The migrations and the ensuing demographic growth changed the continental balance of population distribution (Table 1.3 and Figs 1.5, 1.6, and 1.7), although the low density of occupation and rapid exploitation of new environments in the New World has contrasted markedly with the higher densities and longer-term utilization of environments in much of the Old World. The evidence of deforestation in Latin America illustrates this.

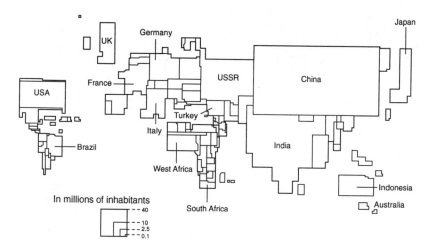

Fig. 1.6 Distribution of population by countries in 1900 (after Noin 1991).

The dominance of Asia in the world population map is still striking, especially East and South Asia which together account for about 48 per cent of the world's population on 4.4 per cent of the Earth. On the other hand, the European population has diminished as a proportion of the world total, and, excluding the former USSR, now comprises less than 10 per cent of the total. In contrast, Africa now accounts for over 12 per cent and, with the highest population growth rates, is rapidly overtaking the Americas.

Equally significant environmentally has been the large-scale urbanization of population, from about 3 per cent in towns of 5000 inhabitants or more in 1800 to 14 per cent in 1900 to 29 per cent in 1950 and about 48 per cent today – much more rapid than total population growth. At least 2½ billion people now live in urban centres (Table 1.4), and many more live in smaller centres with increasingly urbanized facilities, reducing greatly the land-boundedness of people. However, large cities have transformed their environments most. In 1850 there were only three cities (London, Beijing, and Paris) with more than a million inhabitants, but 100 years later there were 75 (Lowry 1991). By 2000 half of the world's urban population will be living in cities with one million inhabitants or more. Even more striking has been the growth of mega-cities, megalopoli and urbanized regions with multiple millions of inhabitants, which create entirely new population-environment relationships as they concentrate energy production, transportation networks, secondary and tertiary activities, and the

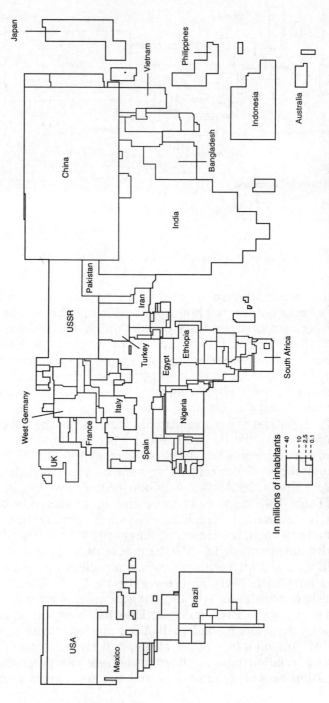

Fig. 1.7 Distribution of population by countries in 1990 (after Noin 1991).

Table 1.4 World population (in billions) by urban and rural residence, 1950–2020

	Urban population	Rural population
1950	0.75	1.82
1960	1.08	1.97
1970	1.36	2.36
1980	1.78	2.70
1990	2.58	2.76
2000 (est.)	3.29	3.01
2010 (est.)	4.09	3.17
2020 (est.)	5.02	3.26

creation of waste and pollutions. There are now more people living in Mexico City or Tokyo than in all urban centres in 1800. By 2000 two-thirds of the 24 cities with 10 million inhabitants or more will be in LDCs, where 49 cities are expected to have a population of over 4 million (see Fig. 1.8 and United Nations 1991), most of them near the coast. Generally, the cost of maintaining environmental quality rises with city size, and the population–environment problems of mega-cities in LDCs are particularly intransigent: loss of agricultural land; greater use of water and energy; extensive slums and shanty-towns; the juxtaposition of industries and housing, sometimes with disastrous results (e.g. Bhopal); air and water pollution; waste disposal; and issues of environmental health.

We must emphasize therefore that apart from the rapid growth of world population, there is growing concentration of population in economic core areas on smaller areas of the Earth's surface, and this process is ongoing through natural increase and in-migration, especially in LDCs. Most economic core areas tend to be close to the coast, so that it is estimated that nearly two-thirds of the world's population live within 60 km of the coast, three-quarters of them living within tropical developing countries (UNCED 1991), often in deltaic and low-lying areas where seas become excessively polluted and coastlines are vulnerable to oscillations in sea level (Fig 1.9). In contrast, there has been little colonization of the uninhabited and sparsely inhabited harsher environments occupying 35–40 per cent of the Earth's area. They have experienced more outward than inward migration as they become more marginalized from the world economy.

Although population concentration is increasing, we should stress that environmental degradation is not directly correlated with

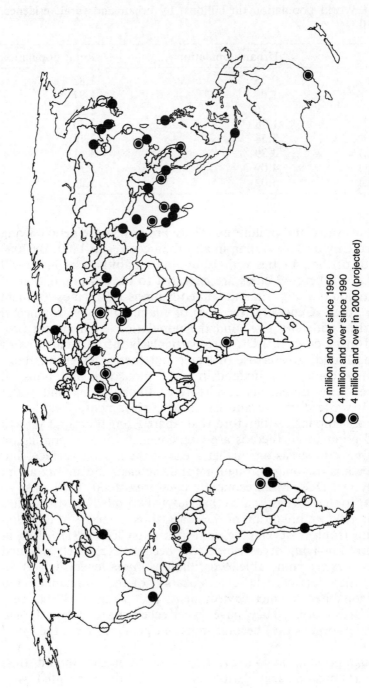

Fig. 1.8 Largest urban areas in the world in 1950, 1990, and 2000. (Source: Population Reference Bureau.)

○ 4 million and over since 1950
● 4 million and over since 1990
◉ 4 million and over in 2000 (projected)

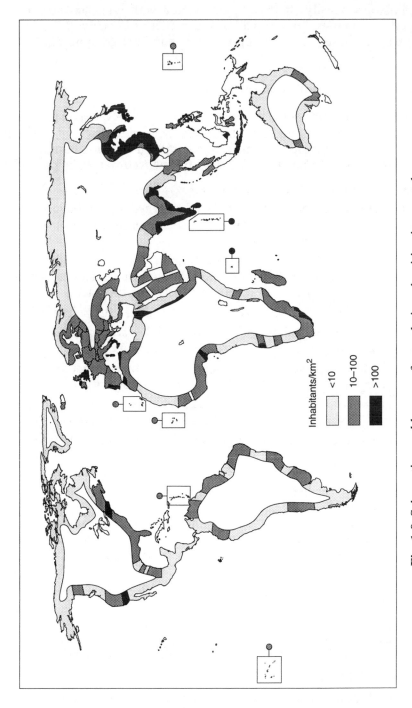

Fig. 1.9 Schematic world map of population densities in coastal areas. (Source: *Times World Atlas.*)

population density. It may be associated with high densities as in many mega-cities, but also with low densities as in many of the desert fringes. So much depends upon other non-demographic factors.

Socio-economic and political changes

These huge demographic changes have been closely associated with, and sometimes triggered by, numerous socio-economic and political changes, whose relative significance is difficult to disentangle. The following list summarizes a complex interwoven web (Clarke 1989):

- accelerating advances in technology;
- dramatic changes in sources of energy, which have greatly affected economic and residential locations as well as public and personal mobility;
- transformations in transportation and communications, increasing the volume and rapidity of movement of goods, people, and ideas, affecting the locations of places;
- industrialization, its localization and global diffusion;
- increasing consumption of renewable and non-renewable resources, particularly by richer populations;
- changes in agriculture; its mechanization, commercialization, crop varieties, livestock breeds, and productivity;
- growth of the service sector, localized particularly in large cities;
- diffusion of the European state system which has fragmented the world politically by superimposing over a myriad of peoples features such as nationalization of populations through sovereignty over territories, centralized authority, and increasing direct and indirect effects of government policies upon populations;
- marked economic differentiation of countries, leading initially to their dichotomous grouping into more- and less-developed countries (North/South, developed/developing), but subsequently into more complex classifications owing to divergence among LDCs, many becoming industrialized and others experiencing very little growth; and
- growing globalization of markets with the expansion of the capitalist world economy over which there is no single political control, though international organizations are very gradually extending their influence and authority.

This list of changes might be extended, but the essential point

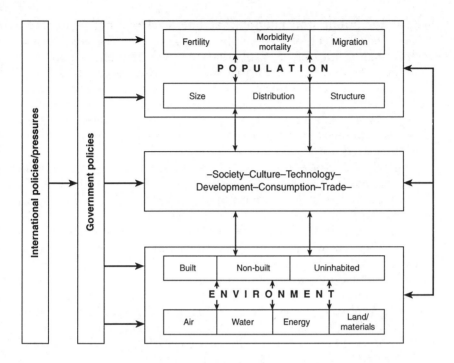

Fig. 1.10 Model of factors intervening between population and environment.

is that they have all intervened to a greater or lesser extent between populations and their environments, so that population–environment interrelationships have become less direct and more indirect, less an ultimate factor (like polluting technologies, warfare, and land mismanagement) than an aggravating factor (Shaw 1989). Fig. 1.10 indicates that the linkages are multidirectional. Moreover, globalization means that populations are increasingly affecting, and are affected by, remote environments and populations; this is particularly true of the most-developed countries which have world-wide impacts, often through transnational companies whose political responsibilities for environments may be minimal. It is suggested by many in the South that the process of dependent development which has evolved with globalization is a direct cause of global environmental change.

MEASURES, LIMITS, AND CRISES

The complexity of population–environment interrelationships is sometimes obscured by over-simplified formulae, which may be helpful for public understanding at one level but not at another. Thus Ehrlich's (1968) formula $1 = P \times A \times T$, where $1 =$ environmental impact, $P =$ population, $A =$ affluence, and $T =$ technology (P and A being mostly indirect/proximate factors and T being mostly direct/ultimate) is useful as a generalization about global impacts, but has less value in the analysis of more local situations (Zaba and Clarke 1994), where P, A, and T are interdependent and where there are many cases of increased environmental degradation associated with declining affluence.

Similarly, the concept of carrying capacity, which is Malthusian in character, has varying utility according to level of analysis. Initially used by biologists in an animal population-supporting sense, it was adapted for studies of human populations (Higgins *et al.* 1982). Unfortunately, it was more useful for traditional societies than modern societies where technology alters resource use and populations are integrated into the world economy. Modern societies are not closed systems, and thus population thresholds of carrying capacity or of optimum population and over-population should never be regarded as absolutes (Brookfield 1976), and should take account of the potential impact of technological change, trade, and other factors (Zaba and Scoones 1994). Estimates of carrying capacity also tend to be imprecise; even the carrying capacity of the Earth as a whole has been variously estimated at between 7.5 and 50 billion.

Recently, the concept of carrying capacity has been increasingly, and perhaps more usefully, used in a more environmental, population-sustaining sense to signify the ability of an area to sustain a population over a long period of time. The idea is not new — William Allan (1965) propounded it nearly 30 years ago — but it is valuable in emphasizing that populations should live off the 'interest' of environmental resources rather than off their 'principal', because renewable resources such as fisheries and forests are not easily replaced.

There are undoubtedly environmental thresholds which once crossed can lead to a 'jump effect' with an abrupt decline in the ability of an area to sustain a population. The jump effect may be associated with a disaster, whose origin may be:

- environmental (e.g. earthquake, volcano, flood, drought, hurricane, tidal wave);
- technological (e.g. nuclear explosion, oil spill, chemical leakage);
- demographic (e.g. population pressure, epidemic);
- economic (e.g. deforestation, mineral and fishery exhaustion); or
- political (e.g. warfare, terrorism, violation of rights, ethnic cleansing).

Combinations of causes including demographic factors have led to some of the more major catastrophes of our time, like the Great Leap Forward in China, the Sahel drought, and the inundations of Bangladesh. Generally, disasters of purely environmental origin cause less loss of life than those of human or multiple origins (Clarke *et al.* 1989).

Disasters are among the crisis issues upon which researchers on population–environment relationships are focusing, others being deforestation, desertification, mega-cities, heavily industrialized regions, and contrasting consumption patterns (CICRED 1992). The identification of crisis areas is an important outcome of this research.

While these crisis issues are of immediate importance, there are of course many long-term issues, some of which may be of even greater significance, including the effects of:

(1) rising population on land management and agricultural productivity;

(2) rising population on water management;

(3) climatic changes on long-term population distribution;

(4) migration and urbanization on the environment;

(5) environmental change on migration;

(6) pollution and environmental degradation on maternal and child morbidity and mortality; and

(7) population growth on local biodiversity through increasing crop specialization and/or loss of wildlife habitats.

All these crisis and long-term topics have been recommended to demographic research centres around the world (CICRED 1992).

PERCEPTIONS, POVERTY, AND POLICIES

We have portrayed a world with extremely diverse populations living in diverse environments and influenced to a greater or lesser extent by a wide variety of technological, economic, social, and political processes which have affected them and their environments. Inevitably, diverse perceptions and attitudes to population–environment relationships have evolved. The desire of traditional agricultural societies for a symbiotic relationship, ecological equilibrium, and balance with nature is still to be found, especially in many fragile environments where subtle changes can lead to disaster. Adaptations to drought and other environmental difficulties have long been characteristic of such societies (Abernethy, 1979; Mortimore, 1989), which have often suffered from the impact of externally imposed development projects (e.g. dams, power stations, plantations) that have underplayed the need for ecological equilibrium. The growth of population in such societies has sometimes also led to disequilibrium and disaster, but not always. In the Malthusian–Boserupian debate about the negative and positive aspects of growing population pressure, proponents can find evidence for both sides of the argument among food-producing agricultural societies, although probably more of the negative than the positive, as evidenced by the increasing volume of environmentally induced migrants sometimes referred to as environmental refugees. As Falkenmark (1991) has repeatedly stressed, water scarcity is a specific and increasing constraint, especially in Africa, and frequently triggers such migrations. There is little doubt, however, that a population's response to resource pressure is greatly affected by a variety of socio-economic and institutional factors, such as economic growth, poverty, government policies, and infrastructure, and therefore may be multiphasic (Bilsborrow 1992).

It is probably tenable to postulate that as populations develop and urbanize they become less environmentally sensitive to the fragilities of their local environments. Certainly, there are contrasting attitudes about population, environment, and development. Views in LDCs tend to be more local, and the desire for development leads to greater tolerance of environmental degradation, views which were common in the MDCs in the past. Now the more educated public in the MDCs are more globally aware, experiencing movements towards post-materialism, greater greenness, and declining individualism, and generally they accept that population growth plays an important role in environmental problems and vice versa. Of course, views vary greatly from country to country, from group to group, by age and sex, and between people, planners, and politicians.

The underlying North–South divide manifested itself again at the UN Conference on Environment and Development (UNCED) at Rio de Janeiro in 1992. There MDCs and LDCs gave quite different weightings to economics, finance, consumption, and population as causes of environmental stress (Grubb *et al.* 1993). LDCs repeatedly made the point that one-sixth of the world's population living in rich countries accounted for about three-quarters of the world's gross product and trade, and were the cause of most of the global environmental problems. On the other hand, the poorest fifth receive only 1.4 per cent of the global income and 1.3 per cent of global investment (Myers 1993). They stressed that much of their own environmental degradation results from poor people searching for basic essentials — food, water, fuel, and fodder — that poverty leads to out-migration, and that the poor suffer from unhealthy environments because of inadequate sanitation, housing, water supply, and waste disposal, all of which contribute to the persistent prevalence of environmental diseases. So naturally countries of the South felt that the poor (an ill-defined population group) should be targeted with investments for the environment, education, and health.

In contrast, many countries of the North were dissatisfied that 'demographic dynamics and sustainability' constituted only 1 of the 40 chapters in Agenda 21, the action plan for the elusive target of sustainable development, and felt that insufficient emphasis had been given to reduction in population growth through family planning and contraception, partly because of Catholic-inspired opposition, notably by the Vatican.

Consequently, demographic emphasis was more on rather longer-term issues such as reproductive choice, family security, child mortality, women's rights, and access to reproductive health techniques than on population control. Although improved access to contraceptive technology would be one of the cheapest measures to improve the overall situation, for many LDCs it smacks too much of authoritarian population control and doomsday scenarios.

In the preparation for the intergovernmental International Conference on Population and Development to be held in Cairo in September 1994, it appears that although individual countries have particular concerns over issues such as abortion and international migration, there is a growing consensus that population matters have to be treated in an integrated manner with social and economic development and the environment, that population is not an optional extra, and that a balance has to be achieved between them.

Intergovernmental conferences tend to produce numerous recommendations which are lost in the sands of time, but they have to try to exact a political commitment from sovereign states so that specific actions are taken at national level. The countries of the South want more than programmes to reduce their rates of population growth, urbanization, and environmental deterioration, and to improve human rights especially for women; they want a commitment not merely to sustained development but also to sustained economic growth along with an improvement in the quality of life for all peoples through reduction in poverty and better health, sanitation, and housing. In brief, issues of population, development, and environment must be dealt with together. The challenge is monumental, but can only really be handled at national level where, unfortunately, friction is still great and is being fanned by the flames of ethnicity. The much-desired 'peace divider' would be extremely beneficial in reducing massive over-expenditure on armaments and releasing funds for other purposes, but the current omens are not very encouraging.

REFERENCES

Abernethy, V. (1979). *Population pressure and cultural adjustment.* Human Sciences Press, New York.

Allan, W. (1965). *The African husbandman.* Oliver and Boyd, Edinburgh.

Bilsborrow, R. (1992). Population growth, internal migration, and environmental degradation in rural areas of developing countries. *European Journal of Population,* **8**, 125–48.

Brookfield, H. C. (1976). On the notion of population thresholds. In *Population at microscale* (ed. L. A. Kosinski and J. W. Webb). New Zealand Geographical Society, Auckland.

CICRED (1992). *Population and environment.* CICRED, Paris.

Clarke, J. I. (1972). Geographical influences upon the size, distribution, and growth of human populations. In *The structure of human populations* (ed. G. A. Harrison and A. J. Boyce), pp. 17–31, Clarendon, Oxford.

Clarke, J. I. (1976). Population and scale: some general considerations. In *Population at microscale* (ed. L. A. Kosinski and J. W. Webb). New Zealand Geographical Society, Auckland.

Clarke, J. I. (1989). A quarter of a millennium of world population movements, 1780–2030. *Espace, Populations, Sociétés,* Lille, **3**, 295–304.

Clarke, J. I. and Rhind, D. W. (1992). *Population data and global environment change.* ISSC/UNESCO Series 5, Paris.

Clarke, J. I. Curson, P., Kayastha, S. L., and Nag, P. (ed.) (1989). *Population and disaster.* Basil Blackwell, Oxford.

Ehrlich, P. (1968). *The population bomb.* Ballantine, New York.

Falkenmark, M. (1991). Rapid population growth and water scarcity: the predicament of tomorrow's Africa. In *Resources, environment and population: present knowledge, future options* (ed. K. Davis and M. S. Bernstam). A supplement to Vol. 16 *Population and development review* (1990). Oxford University Press, New York.

Goldscheider, C. (1971). *Population modernization and social structure.* Little, Brown, Boston.

Goudie, A. (1984). *The nature of the environment.* Basil Blackwell, Oxford.

Goudie, A. (1993). Environmental uncertainty. *Geography,* **78**, 137–41.

Grubb, M., Koch, M., Thomson, K., Munson, A., and Sullivan, F. (1993). *The 'Earth Summit' agreements: a guide and assessment.* Earthscan, London.

Higgins, G., Kassam, A., Naiken, G., Fischer, G., and Shah, M., (1982). *Potential population supporting capacity of lands in the developing world.* FAO, Rome.

Lowry, I. S. (1991). World urbanization in perspective. In *Resources, environment and population: present knowledge, future options* (ed. K. Davis and M. S. Bernstam). A supplement to Vol. 16 *Population and development review* (1990). Oxford University Press, New York.

Lutz, W. (ed.) (1991). *Future demographic trends in Europe and North America. What can we assume today?* Academic Press, London.

Lutz, W. (ed) (1994). *Population development–environment: understanding interactions on Mauritius.* IIASA in collaboration with University of Mauritius, Laxenburg.

Mortimore, M. (1989). *Adapting to drought. Farmers, famines and desertification in West Africa.* Cambridge University Press, Cambridge.

Myers, N. (1993). Population, environment, and development, *Environmental Conservation*, **20**, 205–16.

Noin, D. (1991). *Atlas de la Population Mondiale.* Reclus-La Documentation Française, Paris.

Shaw, R. P. (1989). Rapid population growth and environmental degradation: ultimate versus proximate factors. *Environmental Conservation*, **16**, 199–208.

Tabah, L. (1992). Population growth in the Third World. In *Science and sustainability: selected papers on IIASA's 20th anniversary.* Vienna, International Institute for Applied Systems Analysis.

UNCED (1991). Relationship between demographic pressures, unsustainable consumption patterns, development and environmental degradation. Doc. A/CONF. 151/PC/46.

United Nations (1991). *World urbanization prospects.* UN, New York.

Wahren, C. (1991). Population, environment, development: an inseparable troika. *Populi*, **18**, 4–23.

Zaba, B. and Clarke, J. I. (1994). Introduction: current directions in population–environment research. In *Environment and population change* (ed. B. Zaba and J. I. Clarke). Ordina, Liège.

Zaba, B. and Scoones, I. (1994). Is carrying capacity a useful concept to apply to human populations? In *Environment and population change* (ed. B. Zaba and J. I. Clarke). Ordina, Liège.

2

Population and environment—our nature and our fate: an evolutionary perspective

Geoffrey Harrison

Professor Geoffrey Ainsworth Harrison held a personal Chair in Biological Anthropology at Oxford University from 1976 until his retirement in 1994 and has been a Fellow of Linacre College since 1965. He has the unusual distinction of holding first degrees from both Cambridge (Trinity College) in natural sciences and archaeology and anthropology, and Oxford (Christ Church) in zoology. He also holds a B.Sc. from the University of London, and was awarded his Doctorate at Oxford in 1954. In that year Geoffrey Harrison was appointed to a lectureship in human anatomy at the University of Liverpool, where he stayed until 1963 when he returned to Oxford as Reader in Physical Anthropology and head of the anthropology laboratory. His fieldwork has taken him to south-west Africa, Ethiopia, Brazil, New Guinea, and Australia. His publications include The structure of human populations *(1972) and* Population structure and human variation *(1977). The creation of a statutory Professorship of Biological Anthropology in the University of Oxford from 1994 testifies to the recognition that Geoffrey Harrison has won for his subject as a key discipline among the human sciences.*

Seen from the viewpoint of practically every other species there are just too many human beings. The most recent estimate is around $5\frac{1}{2}$ billion. Many other plants and animals can more than match that number, but they are all small in size. Nothing else comes near to the amount of biomass 'locked up' in *Homo sapiens*. Only a relatively few human parasites and commensals benefit from that.

The impact of the species number on natural ecosystems has been enormous and does not need substantial documentation here. Every part of the Earth's land surface has been markedly affected except Antarctica, and most marine and atmospheric zones have been modified. Wilderness is fast disappearing: there is now almost nothing that can be called virgin forest, certainly in equatorial and tropical ecosystems, all of which have been much influenced by human activity. Only in a few remote temperate regions such as the southern tip of South Island, New Zealand and Tasmania has forest not been profoundly changed. Inevitably more people means more pollution, more environmental damage, and more extinctions of other species.

Large numbers are not even necessarily beneficial to the human species. They have certainly provided exceptional opportunities for disease agents, and there seems to be a true 'adaptive radiation' of viruses resulting from high human density and geographical mobility. Crowding is not perceived as desirable by most human beings and the kinds of society that have typically been generated by big groups seem to be characterized by anomie, aggression, stress, control and bureaucracy, and various other public and private unpleasantnesses or morbidities.

It is true that fertility rates have dropped considerably in recent years as a result of active family planning and improved education in most parts of the world outside Africa and the Middle East. But the decline now seems to have slowed considerably. In part this is due to structural factors, such as age pyramids with a high proportion of people in the Third World in their reproductive years as a result of past population fertility. But in most countries fertility is well above replacement levels, and with such an enormous baseline even a small growth rate represents an enormous number of extra people. Taking a somewhat longer view than most, but still short in evolutionary time, Parkes (1993) estimates that were recent growth rates to continue for 1000 years there would then be '1700 people to each square yard of the earth's surface—land and sea'. This is obviously not a prediction, just an indication of the pressure of current human reproduction.

However, large numbers are relatively new in human experience. The hominid family probably originated over 5 million years ago. Modern humans, in the sense of peoples who were anatomically essentially identical to ourselves, arose around 200 000 years ago. Throughout almost all of this evolutionary history hominids were scarce. For some four-fifths of their existence they were confined to the African savannah and probably comprised no more than a few thousand individuals at any one time. For various reasons, and particularly the small starting base, it is easy to underestimate the global growth rate, but throughout the whole of the Palaeolithic and Mesolithic one might well have wondered if the hominid lineage were going to persist.

The situation began to change quite strikingly with the onset of the Neolithic and the beginnings of agriculture and the domestication of animals. These seminal events, of course, began to liberate human populations from the constraints of natural food resources. They started in the Middle East around 10 000 years ago but were much later in many places and, indeed, can hardly be said to have reached Australia until after the European discovery.

There was clearly a surge in population growth with the adoption of neolithic economic practices, but the demographic evidence strongly suggests that the size of most populations soon came more or less to a state of equilibrium. Such a view tends to be supported by observation today of societies who maintain fully traditional systems, where there is little evidence of growth. The now widely-observed phenomenon of 'population explosion' is quite recent and largely associated with new events such as urbanization, industrialization, modernization, and mass human movements.

Prior to the neolithic revolution, and for many for a long time after it, human beings thus lived in relatively small social groups. During the Palaeolithic and Mesolithic, the mode of subsistence was a so-called 'hunter–gatherer' one in which humans did no more than take from the natural environment what that environment offered in terms of food and other needs. In the later part of the Palaeolithic hunting and fishing became a main source of food for some peoples. This required the development of quite sophisticated weaponry. For most of human history, however, gathering seems to have been the activity which provided most of the food. Gathered food was mainly of the vegetable kind, but there is a view that scavenging was also important in earliest times.

Attempting to reconstruct the habits and economies of early hominids and researching the lifestyles and social organization of the few remaining peoples who are 'hunter–gatherers' may seem a rather esoteric exercise, far removed from the problems of the modern world. But if we are to understand our nature, or at least the biological components of our nature, it is vital that we do just this. Our biological nature is surely a cause, if not the primary cause, of our current problems, specifically those of population and environment, but most others also. We are essentially a product of our biological evolution. For almost the whole of that evolution, 5 million years or so, we were hunter–gatherers. The time that has elapsed since even the earliest Neolithic, and particularly since modernization, is, in evolutionary terms, trivially short.

The examination of the problems of current human ecology from an evolutionary perspective has been undertaken in most detail by Stephen Boyden (1970). He predicted the kinds of morbidities we might expect to find today as a consequence of the possession of characteristics which were evolved as adaptations to one kind of environment — that experienced by hunter-gatherers — but which are inappropriate to the vastly different ones experienced by most people today. He termed these characteristics 'phylogenetic mal-adjustments' — an obvious misnomer but eminently memorable. A clear example is the flight-fight response and its endocrinological catecholamine base, which is surely adaptive to hunter-gatherer lifestyles but is often elicited in inappropriate circumstances today where there is no opportunity for the anticipated levels of physical activity (such as sitting in a traffic jam), and which has been invoked as contributing to cardiovascular and other disease. Boyden pre-dicted the nutritional health dangers of high saturated fat intake, low cellulose intake, high salt intake and substitution of human milk by cows' milk for the feeding of infants, solely by comparison of modern diets with those traditional in hunter-gatherer societies. He identified these dangers when there was little or no direct epidemio-logical evidence, demonstrating the value of the approach. I par-ticularly want to use it for considering some aspects of population, especially human fertility.

Unfortunately, relevant evidence is not as good as one would wish. The archaeological record, by its nature, can provide very little, and one is largely left with examining present-day hunter-gatherers. Such groups as the San peoples of southern Africa and Australian Abo-rigines are now rare; they tend to have survived only in particularly harsh environments like the Kalahari and Australian deserts and, notwithstanding remoteness, have almost all been affected to some degree in recent years by contact with outside groups. On the other hand, some peoples with other traditional economies, such as swid-den cultivators and pastoralists, continue to show some behaviours which are not all that different to those of hunter-gatherers, and study of their behaviours can help us to understand ancestral reproductive behaviours, as well as the impact of economic change.

The outstanding feature of the demography of modern hunter-gatherers and many simple agriculturalists is that populations, prior to contact, appear to have been more or less stable. In part this was surely due to high mortality rates, especially of infants. But it was also due to the intriguing fact that fertility was not particularly high. The total number of babies born to mothers who have survived to menopausal age is a good simple measure of the fertility of women. The individual record appears to be 67, but average population values can be over 11, as among present Hutterites in the USA. Yet the mean figures for hunter-gatherers, hunters, and many simple cultivators tend to be around 3 to 5.

One of the best estimates was made by Nancy Howell (1979) for the Dobe !Kung of the Botswana Kalahari. In 62 women who were aged 45 or more the mean parity was 4.69 yet, surprisingly, many women had had at least one child. A recent analysis of Herero pastoralists in South Africa indicates that total fertility was as low as 2.65 in the first half of this century (Pennington and Harpending 1993), although venereal disease may have played a significant role in this exceptionally low rate. Among the Gaing, a swidden cultivator group in Papua New Guinea, the value is 4.3 (Wood 1993). These are among the most accurate estimates, but similar values have been obtained in other groups (Campbell and Wood 1988).

Fertility rates are influenced by many factors, both biological and cultural. A number of these vary by individual and population circumstance, and will be considered shortly. But one of the most important factors to affect human reproduction is a unique species characteristic: concealed ovulation and constant sexual receptivity in the female. In all other mammals females clearly signal to males, by various physiological and behavioural means, the time when copulation is most likely to lead to fertilization. In humans this just does not occur at all, or does so to a very minimal degree. Women themselves appear to have little or no knowledge of ovulation time, which can only be established through careful physiological monitoring. There has been much speculation about the evolutionary causes for this phenomenon, focusing on the advantages of human pairbonding for our past ecology. The causes need not concern us here, but concealed ovulation has profound consequences for reproductive behaviour and fertility, however it may have arisen. With what in essence is very much a 'hit or miss' affair, fertilization and conception depend upon frequent and regular mating throughout more or less the whole of the female reproductive cycle. Seen solely from the immediate reproductive viewpoint the system seems highly inefficient when compared with what happens in other mammals, and some endocrinologists have expressed surprise that with such a system humans are actually as fertile as they are. However, all depends upon the frequency of mating.

It has been shown, particularly by Roger Short (1988), how the anatomy of humans and their closest relatives, the Great Apes, is related to mating behaviour. For their body size, the testes and accessory reproductive system of the orang-utan and gorilla are comparatively small; they mate infrequently. The chimpanzee has particularly large testes, accounted for by its promiscuous behaviour and the inevitable sperm competition that occurs when many males mate with a single female who is in heat. Those animals who produce the most sperm are likely to be the most successful in reproduction. Human testis size is intermediate, but penis size is outstandingly greater; these are adaptations to frequent mating with a particular female, not only throughout her cycle, but also throughout the whole year, since there is no distinct breeding season. Short, incidentally, concludes that human beings, by nature, are 'serially monogamous'.

Later, the issue of the relevance of this 'nature' to present population problems will be considered further, but first some of the features that are responsible for variation in reproductive performance between human individuals and groups should be examined.

Prior to the advent of reliable means of contraception, by far the most important biological regulator of female fertility was breast-feeding. Suckling by the infant initiates a quite complex sequence of physiological processes which act to suppress ovulation. The most important regulator of these processes is the frequency and length of feeding episodes. The form of the nipple stimulation produced by the suckling also appears to be important. The occurrence of the process is demonstrated by the well-known phenomenon of lactational amenorrhoea, in which many women have no menstrual periods during at least the first part of their breast-feeding, and ovulation may not immediately return on the resumption of menses. In many traditional societies, and especially hunter–gatherer ones, breast-feeding is continued, as a frequent behaviour, for many months post-partum, and children as old as 3 or 4 years are put to the breast, especially if there has been no further birth. One reason for the prolonged breast-feeding is the unsuitability of many of the available natural foods for the feeding of infants. Even after cooking, these tend to need chewing. Babies do not erupt any teeth until about 6 months of age, and the full infant complement is not present until about 2 years. However, one could also argue that late tooth eruption is an adaptation to breast-feeding, and at least as important as the nutritional dimension is the reproductive one of ovulatory suppression. The evolutionary significance of this is that it generates a substantial interval between successive births. Paradoxically, birth spacing favours reproductive success. For nomadic hunter-gatherers, the responsibility for more than one fully dependent infant places an excessive load upon a mother, and both maternal and child survival are dependent upon appropriate spacing. The value of such spacing to the Kalahari San has been demonstrated, for example, by Blurton-Jones and Sibly (1978) in terms of the energetics and heat load of carrying infants. San women incidentally carry young infants with them wherever they go, partly at least, one presumes, because this allows the frequent breast-feeding which helps maintain infertility.

A number of other biological circumstances affect fertility.

Maternal nutritional status has clearly been shown to be important in a number of ways. Perhaps most significant is its effect on growth and physical maturation. In a number of traditional societies, menarche—the age of first menstrual bleeding and a quite good indicator of reproductive maturity—is late. Among the Gaing, for example, the median age is 18.4 years, and among Sherpas of Nepal between 17 and 19. In western Europe, on the other hand, menarcheal age has been systematically falling over the past 100 years or more, and in Britain today is about 13 years or less, on average. Similar trends have also been occurring in other developed societies and are now apparent in some developing ones.

Although a number of factors may have contributed, improving nutrition is almost certainly the main one. There is, in fact, some quite strong evidence that a girl does not become reproductively mature until she has deposited a critical amount of body fat, which will help her meet the additional energy costs of pregnancy and lactation. It has also been suggested that birth spacing may be affected by the time it takes for the restoration of some fat reserves: a process that is clearly nutritionally dependent. Also, starvation, and related morbidities such as anorexia, are associated with amenorrhoea and fertility loss. A fall in age of menarche of the order of magnitude observed clearly has a significant effect on the length of the reproductive life of a woman, and is thus an important component of a population's fecundity. Variations in breast-feeding, pregnancy number, and menarcheal age can have a profound effect upon the frequency of menstrual cycles. It has been estimated (Judson 1993) that as recently as 200 years ago women in the Western world averaged only 30 menstrual cycles in a life time. Today for women with two children it is nearer to 450.

Infectious disease is a further important determinant of both female and male fertility. This is obviously the case for venereal diseases, which have caused dramatic reductions in the fertility of many populations, but it is also true, to a degree, of infections that are not specifically directed at the reproductive system. For various reasons, physiological and psychological, the chronically sick have low fertility. So far as a population's demography is concerned, however, the effects of infectious disease are much more evident in determining mortality than fertility.

Another possible biological influence is level of physical work. It is well established that high levels of exercise, such as those practised by long-distance runners and some other professional athletes, frequently leads to female amenorrhoea. The mechanisms involved appear to show some common pathways with lactational amenorrhoea. It is less clear that the workloads associated with ordinary life have any effect. There is evidence that the heavy activity of foraging plays a significant role in the low fecundity of female San (Bentley 1985), and in many traditional agricultural societies physical work for women is extremely heavy and to all intents and purposes continuous over daylight hours. It has been shown that ovarian hormone output is much lower in these kinds of societies than our own, but how far this is due to work and how far to nutrition is not clear; anyway, there is likely to be a strong interactional relationship between the two.

It may seem paradoxical, if nutrition, disease, and workload are important determinants of fertility, that high fertility and population growth are today often associated with developing countries in which malnutrition is rife, infectious diseases prevalent, and women have to work particularly hard physically. However, the matter is one of reference point. By comparison with most developed societies fertility is certainly high. But that contrast is essentially one of contracepting versus non-contracepting societies. It is more relevant to compare groups in the developing world with non-contracepting, well-nourished and healthy peoples, such as the Hutterites. As already mentioned, the latter tend to have a fertility nearly twice as great as that prevailing in developing societies.

Particular attention has been focused upon biological determinants of fertility since, in a sense, these set the limits; they are the components of the reproductive *nature* of the organism. Within biology, attention has also centred largely on the female since, from a demographic point of view of population growth or decline, it is the reproductive performance of the woman that matters most. However, social and economic factors can, and do, play a vital role in causing variations and fluctuations in a population's fertility, and here the contribution of males is usually significant also. Age of marriage is a particularly important factor since most children in most societies are born within 'wedlock'. Late marriage played a significant role in the decline in European fertility during the nineteenth century (Coleman and Schofield 1986). Clearly, abortion and infanticide, which may be quite widely practised in hunter–gatherer societies, and celibacy, abstinence, and separation can have marked effects. Then there are indications that variant marriage structures, such as polygamy, may play a role.

From time to time there is discussion as to whether traditional societies, consciously or unconsciously, regulate fertility to ensure optimal population sizes. Carr-Saunders (1922) was among the first to argue against the widespread occurrence of Malthusian regulation through famine, pestilence, and war in traditional situations. One problem is the difficulty in the human, as compared with the animal, situation with the concept of optimal population. There is a good deal of evidence to indicate that population pressure is itself an important stimulus to technological innovation, and in particular innovation for greater food production (Boserup 1965). Seen from a social and economic point of view, many traditional societies have been judged to be underpopulated (Douglas 1966).

Mary Douglas has argued that if there is social regulation of fertility, the perceived limiting factors are not bread and water, but rather prestige and status resources, such as 'oysters and champagne'. Regulatory pressures arise when the latter become in short supply. However, even if this is the case, it does not refute the basic hypothesis of social regulation, only that different criteria are being monitored, and shortage of 'oysters and champagne' can perhaps be seen as an early warning of possible later shortages of 'bread and water'. Status is also important in a more general way. Status aspirations are a feature of human beings and there can be little doubt that they have strong biological foundations; they are a feature of organization of all social mammals. The reasons are obvious enough. Individuals of high status occupy the best parts of the environmental heterogeneity and typically behave to make it even better for themselves. This invariably facilitates access to mates and provides the most favourable circumstances for the rearing of offspring. Probably some of the strongest selection pressures in human evolution have been for characteristics that promote status, and such selection, along with social mobility, acts to create the social stratification that occurs in most, if not all, human societies. Until recently it seemed quite likely that variation in social status was infinitely more important than variation in reproductive physiology in determining reproductive success. What, of course, has now happened is the 'de-coupling' of status from reproductive outcomes by the availability of contraception. People who acquire oysters and champagne do not necessarily have large families.

What is the relevance of all of this to the population problems of the modern non-traditional world? So far as the biological determinants are concerned, the goals and aspirations of most peoples, such as improved nutrition and reduced infection, are only likely to increase female fertility — and they will certainly reduce mortality — thus, in themselves, tending to increase population pressure. A reduction in physical work loads may act in a similar direction unless very large numbers of women choose recreational long-distance running, or the like. Breast-feeding should continue to be encouraged everywhere. One of the worst examples of recent Third World exploitation was the widespread promotion of cows' milk baby foods as substitutes for breast-feeding in poorly educated societies. But the merits of breast-feeding are primarily in its effects on infant and maternal health and well-being. Any decrease in fertility is likely to be considerably offset by a reduction in mortality, so more breast-feeding could actually lead to more population growth.

Biological mechanisms, not surprisingly, are pro-natalist. They highlight the essential role that contraception must play if healthy populations are ever going to stabilize to acceptable sizes. However, contraceptive technology of itself is never likely to be enough. Even if the perfect contraceptive were always to hand at no cost to every individual, fertility might well be excessive. What really matters is the willingness or desire of people to use such contraception. Here again human biology works to defeat the control of fertility. In other mammals reproduction is ensured solely through sexual behaviour. In humans, however, there is an additional dimension: a conscious desire to have children. Neville Bruce (1989) has termed this the 'pro-creative urge' and sees it as an inherent biological drive which, in the framework of human consciousness, can help compensate for the 'hit and miss' nature of human mating. Thus many people have sex not only because it is enjoyable but also because they want children. It does not really matter from a demographic point of view whether this 'wanting' is fundamentally biological or not. It certainly appears to be at a high frequency in women in all societies and effectively universal in most. Relevant systematic evidence is scarce, but I have asked women of all reproductive ages and many parities in various traditional and acculturating societies whether they want a(nother) child and never once been given the answer 'no'. How far this is an 'expected' response it is obviously impossible to say; and it probably does not matter, since in these societies cultural expectation is usually individual practice, and for many people in these situations there are numerous advantages in having a large number of children. Care in old age is invariably important, and a larger work force is frequently useful in subsistence activities and outweighs the increased nutritional demand. Then power and prestige may often be enhanced by being a member of a large kinship group. High fertility has also to be seen as some protection against the uncertainties from mortality. Under such circumstances there need to be strong incentives to reduce this fertility. China has been quite successful by imposing severe social penalties on those couples who have more than one child, but it is unlikely that this mechanism would be anything like so successful under other political and bureaucratic systems. One would, anyway, prefer more persuasion and less coercion. The usual Western view is that economic development will achieve fertility reduction as it appeared to do in the history of Europe. But the basis for the 'demographic transition' that occurred in Europe has little in common with the situation in the developing world today. Even in Europe economic factors may not have dominated reproductive decisions. A surprising feature of the decline in marital fertility there is that it occurred almost simultaneously over much of the continent in all kinds of economies and in all kinds of social groups. It is suggested that changing 'ideology', if not fashion, was largely responsible (Coale and Watkins 1986).

On the other hand, it does seem to be true today that when child mortality is low many people willingly give up having some babies so that they can afford washing machines and motor cars. I do not think that the causes for this are fully understood. Time- and effort-saving and status-seeking are clearly important, but they do not seem to explain very much of 'shopping behaviour' and the near universal desire to collect things. It is almost as if there were some 'squirrel gene' inherited from our hunter–gatherer past, when collection and storage may have had important survival value. This may be but fanciful speculation, but if there were relatively cheap material objects for which people would willingly reduce their fertility it would be of immense help to population problems!

As it is, the benefits for population growth of attempted economic development have not been impressive. This is partly because so little of any wealth generated nationally filters through to the mass of the population. There are numerous accounts from Third World countries of families who have practised family limitation to provide better education and other opportunities for their children, but who find that there is no employment for these children when they grow up. Such experiences generate intense frustration, if not anger, and a strong desire to return to the 'old system'.

It is also important to emphasize here that even if economic development helps in controlling population growth, and damage to the environment from that growth, economic development as such, at least of the kind we have so far experienced, has not protected the environment at all. Far from it: the global damage done by the First World through pollution and resource destruction in economic development far outweighs, as yet, the environmental damage done by overpopulation in the Third World. 'Sustainable' economic development may well be the solution in both situations, but as has been pointed out endlessly of late, definition of just what 'sustainable' is, and details of how it can be introduced, present innumerable problems.

I trust I have shown that our biological nature—for good evolutionary reasons—is a formidable obstacle to achieving acceptable population levels, both globally and locally. We may be able to modify it sufficiently by social and economic process to avoid Malthusian disaster, but this is far from certain. Some other evolutionary components may help.

Although it is only casually documented in the ethnographic literature, there is no doubt at all that modern hunter–gatherer groups are immensely aware of their environments. Knowledge of natural history is encyclopaedic, and practically every grown-up person is expert in the identification and taxonomy of local plants and animals. Often the plants, animals, and landscape become part of the folklore and mythology, endowed with supernatural and divine properties. It seems likely that this was generally the case throughout 5 million years of human evolution, for survival surely depended upon environmental knowledge, and all activity, lifestyles, and habits were dictated or influenced by environmental factors. Under such circumstances it would not be surprising if biological mechanisms, probably but not necessarily genetic, were established which furthered environmental awareness and appreciation. Mere 'cognition' would facilitate the awareness but appreciation needs something more. Perhaps then in all human beings there is an intrinsic desire to protect the environment. The fact that many may not show it does not invalidate the hypothesis. Even simple genetic traits can be completely suppressed by environmental alteration or manipulation. If, however, such a mechanism is biologically present, then it should be possible to elicit it everywhere with appropriate education and under appropriate circumstances. Clearly, when it comes to a choice between protecting an environment and avoiding starvation, the food-seeking mechanisms win, which at least partly explains why environmental movements tend to be 'middle class'. But if there is a universal potential for environmental caring then our fate may not be so dire. However, ways of fostering it will still need to be found, although the widespread desire for, and joy of, gardening in all economic groups in developed societies suggests this would not be difficult.

Two other features which may be in our nature as a function of our evolutionary history are relevant here. As I have already noted, human groups throughout most of human history were small, probably consisting, like hunter–gatherers today, of no more than an extended family or a few related families. Social experience was certainly small scale, and one would therefore predict that human groups operate most comfortably when they are small. It is not easy to find sound empirical evidence for this, partly because of the difficulty of measuring 'comfort' or whatever other subjective feeling of success one wishes to take. Then there is the difficulty that group size co-varies with a myriad of other behavioural and social circumstances. Common experience also identifies the difficulties that arise when incompatible people cannot escape from one another. But such experience also indicates that people 'get on better' with those they know than with those they don't; that social networks are inversely related to group size, and that social networks can, and do, provide important support structures in societies. These support structures have been shown to be important in health and well-being. If 'small is beautiful' at the level of interpersonal relations then mechanisms need to be developed which will foster community structures, whether these be at home, in the workplace, or in other social life situations. Sets of microcosms for living are not incompatible with the economic and political pressures which are bound to encourage large-scale organizations. A special further advantage of small community structure is that it tends to tie groups of people to particular environments which they come to identify as their own and therefore corporately protect. There are plenty of examples of this in environmental protection groups which are behaving much as hunter–gatherers would. Nor is this kind of structure incompatible with information dissemination or acceptance of social and political change. Even before the time of modern information technologies, ideas could spread extremely rapidly, as is evidenced in the rapid decline in marital fertility across Europe in the nineteenth century.

The second relevant feature from our evolutionary past also concerns behaviour. A fact frequently commented on in the ethnographic literature is the high level of co-operation that occurs in hunter–gatherer groups. Since, as already mentioned, these groups are frequently made up of close biological kin, such co-operation would be expected from kin-selection theory. However, at least in some cases the co-operation appears to extend beyond kin ties. Among San-bushman hunters, hunting skill is much valued, but a successful hunter is invariably modest and diffident about his achievements. The most desirable pieces of his 'kill' are typically offered to other families and he is the last to eat. The evolutionary explanation for what nowadays may seem abnormal behaviour is that hunting success always depends to some extent upon co-operation of all the men in the hunting group, and no-one, however skilful, can afford to alienate through envy any of his colleagues. On their own no-one would be successful. Phenomena such as this are widespread in social mammals and fall broadly under the category of reciprocal altruism in sociobiology theory. There have been difficulties in the theory of collaborative work, sometimes known as the 'prisoner's dilemma', and well exemplified by the problem of comparative effort that the two riders of a tandem bicycle will make. The problem can be circumvented, however, if you have the choice of who you will ride with (Milinski 1993). The main point I want to make here, however, is that co-operative behaviour is as much a part of our evolutionary heritage as competitive behaviour. In many modern societies the competitive element has been greatly encouraged for economic and political purposes, but our very sociability fundamentally depends upon the co-operative elements. In some walks of life this is well enough recognized as, for example, in the military and in team sport, but it needs to be nurtured in many others, and perhaps most of all in education. With increased levels of co-operation many of the problems of the modern world, including excessive population growth and environment destruction, might be more manageable.

The logistic problem comes from consideration of the scale of the co-operating units. Although there is a strong evolutionary basis for co-operativeness between members of the same group, there is none for co-operativeness between groups. Indeed, such biology as there is in intergroup relations will tend to act to generate hostility. This may well play a part in the ethnic violence and widespread racism which plagues the world today. However, there is nothing immutable in the definition of groups, and individuals can change their perception of the nature and size of the group to which they belong. Throughout most of human evolution a group was basically identified as a set of kin living and working together, but the conception was easily extended to membership of the same tribe, city, and now nation, within which genetic relationships may be very loose. With the power of the modern media it must surely be extendable further and possibly even globally, although one important factor in the fostering of group identity is the presence of another threatening group. Come an attack from outer space, we would quickly develop a 'brotherhood of man'! Nevertheless, if the media chose to give more attention to a massacre in Madras than to a bloody nose in Bradford, people would progressively begin to feel more a part of a single world group. One major obstacle to the establishment of family planning campaigns has been the view of a number of national governments, and especially those of relatively small states, that numbers contribute to national power, and birth control campaigns are a form of neo-colonial intervention. It is only when national identities begin to become generally blurred that it will be possible to overcome this obstacle, and trends in this direction are contrary to the expectation that human beings behave best in small groups.

CONCLUSION

Our biological nature is particularly pro-natalist and the availability of technologies which decouple sexual behaviour from reproduction are not likely in themselves to stabilize population growth. Further, improvements in the quality of biological life, such as better nutrition and less disease, are likely to improve fecundity, decrease mortality, and exacerbate the population condition. Economic development may help, if it persuades people to forfeit children for 'goods', and there are strong drives for the status that is now represented in 'goods'. But the cultural and economic conditions in the areas of the modern world with high growth rates are very different from those that created the demographic transition in Europe. And although economic development in itself may operate to solve some population problems, it certainly does not, as yet, have positive effects on the environment. On present regimes it is likely only to make matters much worse. Such hope as there is lies in the cultivation of some other aspects of our nature, such as environmental awareness and co-operative behaviour at every level of social and political organization. Such co-operative behaviour is surely a prerequisite of truly sustainable development. Clearly, education has a critical role to play here. It has been said that contraception and education will together solve the world's population problem — and in due course the environmental and economic ones too. With our nature I am not so optimistic about our fate, at least in evolutionary time. But the human organism is without doubt the most adaptable of all. This adaptability has been the basis of its enormous numerical success. Perhaps it will be sufficient to meet the new and greater challenges, but it will be sorely tested.

REFERENCES

Bentley, G. R. (1985). Hunter–gatherer energetics and fertility. A reassessment of the Kung San. *Human Ecology*, **13**, 79–109.

Blurton-Jones, N. and Sibly, R. M. (1978). Testing adaptiveness of culturally determined behaviour. Do Bushman women maximize their reproductive success by spacing births widely and foraging seldom? In *Human behaviour and adaptation* (ed. V. Reynolds and N. Blurton-Jones). Taylor and Francis, London.

Boserup, E. (1965). *The conditions of agricultural growth: the economics of agrarian change under population pressure.* Aldine, Chicago.

Boyden, S. V. (1970). The impact of civilization on the biology of man.

Australian National University Press, Canberra.

Bruce, N. W. (1989). Sex and social issues: the drive to procreative excess. *Proceedings of Australasian Society for Human Biology*, **2**, 289–303.

Campbell, K. L. and Wood, J. W. (1988). Fertility in traditional societies. In *Natural human fertility. Social and biological determinants* (ed. P. Diggory, S. Teper, and M. Potts). Macmillan Press, London.

Carr-Saunders, A. M. (1922). *The population problem: a study in human evolution*. Clarendon Press, Oxford.

Coale, A. J. and Watkins, S. C. (1986). *The decline of fertility in Europe*. Princeton University Press, Princeton.

Coleman, D. and Schofield, R. (ed.) (1986). *The state of population theory*. Blackwell, Oxford.

Douglas, M. (1966). Population control in primitive groups. *British Journal of Sociology*, **17**, 263–73.

Howell, N. (1979). *Demography of the Dobe !Kung*. Academic Press, New York.

Judson, O. (1993). Towards healthier infertility. *Nature*, **365**, 15–16.

Milinski, M. (1993). Co-operation wins and stays. *Nature*, **364**, 12–13.

Parkes, A. S. (1993). *Backlash*. Parkes Foundation, Cambridge.

Pennington, R. and Harpending, H. (1993). *The structure of an African pastoralist community*. Oxford University Press, Oxford.

Short, R. (1988). On the evolution of human reproduction. *Proceedings of the Australasian Society for Human Biology*, **1**, 5–21.

Wood, J. W. (1993). *Fertility and reproductive biology in human biology in Papua New Guinea* (ed. R. Attenborough and M. Alpers). Oxford University Press, Oxford.

3
Genetic engineering: progress, promises, and precepts
Brian Heap

Professor Brian Heap, CBE, FRS, was Director of the Biotechnology and Biological Science Research Council's (BBSRC, formerly AFRC) Institute of Animal Physiology and Genetics Research at Babraham, Cambridge and Edinburgh and AFRC Director of Science. After graduating and then taking his Ph.D. at the University of Nottingham, Professor Heap moved to the University of Cambridge, where he was awarded the degree of Doctor of Science for his research in 1980. In 1963 he had begun his association with his present Institute, near Cambridge, which was to last over 30 years. After several years at Babraham as a research fellow, Professor Heap became head of the Institute's Physiology Department in 1976 and subsequently Director. Currently, he is senior visiting fellow in the School of Clinical Medicine, University of Cambridge, and Special Professor in the University of Nottingham.

Professor Heap has published numerous papers on reproductive biology and endocrinology and has advised the WHO and the government of the People's Republic of China in these fields. He was elected a Fellow of the Royal Society in 1989 and appointed CBE in 1994.

INTRODUCTION

The impact of the growth rate in the human population on the environment is far outstripping the recovery potential of the Earth, and expectations have been raised that biotechnology, of which genetic engineering is but one component, offers hope for the future. Reports of famine, deforestation, soil degradation, atmospheric and aquatic pollution, and loss of animal and plant species are depressingly common. They are associated with the human population explosion; the population has doubled since 1950 and is set to reach about 7 billion by the year 2020, 9.5 billion in 2050, and a plateau of about 10 billion by the year 2100 (Fig. 3.1). They also reflect the availability of cheap fossil fuel which has facilitated the manipulation of natural systems and resources of the Earth to increase food production, and the effective control of diseases such as malaria, typhoid, and cholera. Since 1950 quadruped livestock have increased

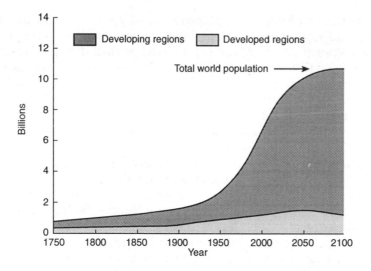

Fig. 3.1 Global population growth in developed and less developed countries (taken from United Nations data).

in numbers from 2 to 4 billion and the fowl population from 3 to 11 billion. During the same period grain production per capita increased by 50 per cent, whereas beef and fish production reached a peak in the early to mid-1970s and subsequently declined because of high costs and overfishing, respectively (Pimentel 1989).

Human population growth rate appears to be following an S-shaped sigmoidal pattern. Theories to explain how contemporary developed countries have progressed through this demographic transition describe three stages:

(1) slow-growing populations with high birth rates and high death rates (before economic modernization);

(2) the transition period with high birth rates and low death rates (with increased modernization leading to decreased mortality and sharp increases in population growth); and

(3) falling birth rates converging with lower death rates leaving little or no population growth (forces of modernization and development leading to a decline in fertility).

In animal populations the braking effect that occurs as numbers approach or exceed the carrying capacity derives from the complex interactions of density-independent factors such as climate, and density-dependent ones, such as access to food and suitable habitats and the impact of parasites, pathogens, and predators (Sinclair 1990; Brown and Rothery 1993). A different pattern of population growth is the J-shaped curve, where exponential growth during favourable conditions is followed by a dramatic, if recoverable, crash resulting from density-dependent destruction of the environment, as in food depletion, or an abrupt change in some density-independent factor, as in the effect of a first frost on the survival of susceptible plants (see Kupchella and Hyland 1986). In early history, humans subsisting by hunting and gathering had to move on or starve as a result of the destruction of vegetation and the depletion of fauna, but the species was too few in number and too dispersed in distribution to cause serious environmental damage. By contrast, in today's world quite small populations can modify the environment in an unparalleled way, which leaves some doubt about the shape of the expected trajectory of global population growth.

Carrying capacity is increasingly recognized to be central to discussions on population and the environment. This was not always the case, probably because the majority 'yearn for a world without limits, and therefore believe that the concept has no validity' (Hardin 1993). The prestigious USA National Research Council's substantial report on population growth and economic development published in 1986 made no mention of carrying capacity. Simon and Kahn (1984) stated that because of increases in knowledge, the Earth's carrying capacity has increased throughout the centuries to such an extent that the term has no meaning. Brundtland (1989) similarly ignored the existence of absolute limits and instead embraced the concept of sustainable development. In contrast, the First World Optimum Population Congress, recently held in Cambridge, focused on how to measure the Earth's carrying capacity, based on food, water, and energy throughput (Daily *et al.* 1993; King and Slessor 1993). The calculations are difficult to formalize since they include judgements about the choice of a tolerable mortality level, evaluation of consumption standards, and the productivity of the environment and its resource base. They aim to determine whether the observed population growth falls within the required objectives to avoid exceeding the carrying capacity (Richardson *et al.* 1993). The significance of carrying capacity needs to be clearly acknowledged; when it is exceeded in 1 year there are serious cumulative consequences in subsequent years because it diminishes progressively the productivity of the environment in question. In Malthusian language, the inevitable consequences of the clash between population growth and food restriction is degradation in the quality of human life, and widespread misery and vice (Malthus 1798).

Malthus (1798) pioneered the connection between economics and population and it was kept alive in the 1850s by John Stuart Mill. Thereafter the subject virtually disappeared from the discipline of economics, and conclusions were reached in the capitalist and former communist worlds that technology and fair distribution would automatically solve the problem. Taboos on issues such as global carrying capacity can be detected repeatedly in the history of the population debate (Hardin 1993); the current debate about global warming is often dominated by physical scientists who seek to monitor the problem, rather than by life scientists who strive to address the biological issues that underlie population growth and its impact on the environment. Equilibrium between mammals and their environment is established by various strategies, including regulation of the time of puberty onset, seasonal breeding, embryonic and fetal mortality, neonatal mortality, and the time interval between successive births. Humans have overcome many of these natural checks and balances by improved nutrition. This has lowered the age at menarche in more-developed countries to less than 13 years, and improved neonatal care has greatly reduced the incidence of infant mortality. On average the annual growth rate for the world population is about 1.7 per cent, with a doubling time of about 40 years. The rate varies greatly from country to country and averages about 2 per cent in developing nations and 0.6 per cent in developed countries. The highest growth rate is in Africa where, at the current rate, the population of the continent will double in 28 years. In Kenya and Zambia the rate is even higher, and the doubling time is only 17 years. In the age structure of these countries there is great potential for continued growth, where for cultural and socio-economic reasons large family size is deemed desirable. The answer to whether we are following a sigmoidal trajectory or a J-shaped curve will therefore depend on many choices, including the success of artificial contraception and the influence of socio-economic and cultural factors. Population growth *will* be checked somehow. The point at issue is when, and by what means, will this be achieved.

FERTILITY

Currently, the artificial regulation of human fertility depends on the use of a limited range of options of differing efficacy, including steroids, barriers, sterilization, and abortifacients. World-wide, over 60 million women use oral contraceptives. In the UK over 50 per cent of women aged between 18 and 44 use the pill, more than 25 per cent rely on condom usage, 12 per cent the IUD, and the remainder depend on various procedures (diaphragm, chemicals, or the natural rhythm method). Since 1983 the overall level of oral contraceptive use has remained fairly stable, but there has been a steady increase in its use by women aged less than 20, and a steady decline in women aged over 35, possibly because of the adverse publicity that the pill is contraindicated in the latter group if they smoke (Drife and Baird 1993). The safety and efficacy of combined oral contraceptives containing a synthetic progestagen and a low dose of oestrogen remain the two most relevant issues to the consumer and research scientist. The constituents of oral contraceptives are highly efficacious and also exert major protective effects, even after their cessation, against ovarian and endometrial cancer (Thorogood and Villard-Mackintosh 1993). Other methods that prevent pregnancy include long-acting injectable preparations of steroids (progestagens alone or in combination with oestrogens) which block cervical mucus penetration, fertilization, endometrium or ovarian function; analogues of the decapeptide gonadotrophin releasing hormone (GnRH) which prevent ovulation; and intrauterine devices that interfere with fertilization and the process of implantation.

Recent successful developments have not ventured far beyond the area of steroid chemistry, and the most notable is the antigestagen, mifepristone (RU486), which blocks the actions of progesterone, the hormone of pregnancy, by binding to the endometrial progesterone receptor. This is one of few new concepts introduced into the area of human fertility control during the past decade and is targeted to inhibit end-organ responses. Controversially, it has been adopted in conjunction with the prostaglandin, sulprostone, as an abortifacient in women with amenorrhoea of less than 63 days (Baird 1993). Because progesterone is important both for implantation and for the maintenance of pregnancy, RU486 may also be effective as an anti-implantation rather than abortifacient (post-implantation) agent.

Pregnancy and its establishment and maintenance are among the most complex of physiological processes in mammals. The power of genetic engineering with recombinant DNA technologies is being adopted to elucidate a range of mechanistic problems associated with early pregnancy and to search for novel target molecules. Immuno-contraception is one possibility that would facilitate pregnancy by choice rather than by chance since a vaccine directed against one or more targets could be used periodically; it would reduce the risk of user failure, and yet be physiological in the sense that it would mobilize the body's own machinery rather than relying on constant medication. Unlike conventional vaccination against infectious pathogens, efficacy must satisfy the needs of both full protection and reversibility in healthy adults. The list of requirements for an acceptable vaccine is extensive, and it is perhaps not surprising that vaccine development for fertility regulation has had a protracted and chequered career (Wang and Heap 1992). Most advanced is the active immunization of women against the β-subunit of human chorionic gonadotrophin (hCG), a 'self' molecule which, when dimerized to a non-self carrier (e.g. α-subunit of ovine luteinizing hormone) and then linked to a non-self carrier such as tetanus toxoid or diphtheria toxoid, produces an effective immunogen for vaccination. Phase II efficacy trials have given promising results, with only one pregnancy during 750 menstrual cycles in women of proven fertility, and with successful reversibility of the procedure (Raghupathy and Talwar 1992). Recombinant DNA techniques are currently being used to improve the quality of the immunogen and the efficiency of its large-scale production. The genes coding for hCG-β have been cloned and expressed in vaccinia virus. The genetically engineered construct consists of a long recombinant vaccinia virus which induces substantial antibody production against chorionic gonadotrophin in rodents and monkeys, but there is a long way to go and many regulatory procedures to complete before the technique could hope to be considered acceptable for general use (Talwar *et al.* 1993).

Laboratory-based studies have investigated other candidate molecules as models for vaccine development (Wang and Heap 1992; Lincoln 1993). They include passive (or active) immunization against progesterone itself, using monoclonal antibodies (or anti-idiotypic antibodies) that have been shown to block implantation effectively (Heap *et al.* 1992). Protein engineering of the antibody's recently characterized binding site provides a strategy for the production of purpose-designed molecules that have either agonist or antagonist activity towards progesterone (Arevalo *et al.* 1993). Egg and sperm surface antigens are further targets for immunocontraception. They comprise zona pellucida glycoproteins such as ZP3, and membrane antigens on spermatozoa that actively migrate from the tail to the sperm head during the maturation process. Antibodies against the sperm molecule or its epitopes will prevent sperm–egg interactions and block fertilization (Aitken *et al.* 1993; Jones *et al.* 1993). Another promising avenue is the identification, using recombinant DNA techniques, of a putative disintegrin–fusion peptide in the sperm membrane which targets integrin receptors on the egg plasma membrane at the time of fertilization. The proposition arising from these results is that synthetic peptides corresponding to the disintegrin domain on sperm membranes may be useful as contraceptives (Blobel *et al.* 1992).

The development of a vaccine that is safe, efficacious, and acceptable is a highly desirable objective, not least for less-developed countries. Yet we are a long way from solving fundamental questions such as knowing how to stimulate sustained immunity over a long period of time. Studies of genetically engineered vaccines, improved adjuvants, and the use of polyvalent vaccines that contain immunogens from different targets are vital to success. However, it is difficult to be sanguine about the prospect of a vaccine or any new contraceptive technology being available before the end of the century in a field that is underfunded, over-regulated, and litigation hypersensitive (Djerassi 1992). The immediate tendency is to use what is available more effectively.

Most people seem willing to spend at least 1 per cent of their disposable income on contraception. In less-developed countries, however, the total cost of family planning as a percentage of foreign aid has actually fallen from 2 per cent in the 1970s to less than 1 per cent today (Potts and Crane 1993). The problem is that in many such countries birth rates have not fallen in proportion to the decline in infant mortality and death rates, even though family size is falling 2–7 times more speedily than in the West at a comparable stage of its demographic transition. The reasons why couples want a small family and the ways in which they achieve their goal are well understood, and include educational and employment opportunities for women, improved income levels for husband and wife, and urbanization, all of which are correlated positively with smaller families. Birth rates among the very poor are also likely to fall where infant mortality is reduced by better public health programmes, where the development of old age and social security systems lessen parental dependence on offspring, and where there is a redistribution of assets from rich to poor (Todaro 1989). Parkes (1993) shows that sophisticated methods of contraception have slowed down the rate of population increase in many countries, especially where family planning is the official policy. In Costa Rica the birth rate was slashed to almost half in 11 years, unlike Nicaragua with its strong Catholic influence where there was merely a shift towards slightly older mothers. Positive methods are in use in some areas such as East Asia and Latin America, but two populous areas, Africa and southern Asia, have least use for contraception, and this results in a huge pool of reproductive potential and high population growth rates. A current controversy is whether the AIDS epidemic in Africa will reduce a 3 per cent per annum population growth before the epidemic to below zero once an endemic situation is attained. Projections show that the difference in population growth rates for a no-AIDS and an AIDS scenario is very steady, ranging from 0.5 per cent in the early 1990s to 0.8 per cent in the early years of the twenty-first century. This small effect on population growth is because of the inherently high fertility level, the rarity of mortality in the young adult population even in regions where overall health status is poor, and the replacement of children that apparently die from common childhood illnesses but were in fact HIV-infected by women who were ignorant of their condition (Mann *et al.* 1992). Other analyses indicate that the observed prevalences of infection in the worst afflicted regions of sub-Saharan Africa are sufficient to reduce current population growth rates to close to, or below, zero in the coming decades (Garnett and Anderson 1993). Possibly the most serious impact of AIDS will be the loss of breadwinners in the population, which will undoubtedly aggravate the problems of food security in already deprived areas (Whitehead 1991).

Family size declines as a result of the use of contraception, abortion, or intercourse abstinence, emphasizing the continuing need for improved access to a range of contraceptive options (Potts and Crane 1993). Were we able to talk with other animals, Hardin (1993) believes it is highly unlikely that we should hear them debating the problem of population growth rates. For them the debate is unnecessary because Nature solves the problem (Sinclair 1990), but the question we face is can we replace Nature's ruthless methods with more agreeable ones of our own?

FOOD SECURITY

A second challenge for the skills of genetic engineering is food security. A humanitarian definition expressed by the Brundtland Commission (1987) perceived it as secure ownership of, or access to, resources, assets and income-earning activities to offset risks, ease shocks, and meet contingencies (World Commission on Environment and Development 1987). For most of the world's population this is a rational interpretation of food security, with the prosperous producing that which is surplus to indigenous needs and the less-developed areas benefiting from its distribution to those areas of scarcity. The modern paradox is exemplified in more-developed countries, such as the UK, where close to 10 million acres now used for farming are likely to be surplus by the year 2000 if the intensification of agricultural productivity continues. This trend is associated with costly agricultural support systems in the EU. In contrast, Africa is the only continent failing to keep food production ahead of population growth.

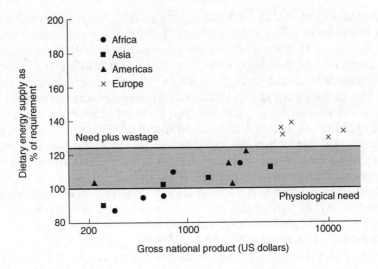

Fig. 3.2 The statistical relationship between GNP per capita of different countries in the world and the sufficiency of their dietary energy supplies. The shaded area represents the estimated physiological requirement (lower limit) and after allowing for a realistic level of food wastage (upper limit; see Whitehead 1991).

Thus, the correlation between gross national product (GNP) and the dietary energy supply shows that certain African countries have the lowest GNP and the lowest dietary energy supply relative to their needs (Fig. 3.2). Africa's population growth rate is far in excess of current rates of increase in indigenous food production and exceeds the potential for improvement within existing agricultural strategies. Subclinical malnutrition exists all the time in many of the less-developed countries, and the World Health Organization estimates that about 100 million children in the world currently have moderate or severe protein–energy malnutrition. Infant mortality in the 34 lowest-income countries, including China, is 114 per 1000 live births, whereas in the UK it is only 11 per 1000 live births (Whitehead 1991).

Food security in less-developed countries can be assured by bringing new lands into production, by increasing yields from already productive land, or by improving use and reducing spoilage of existing food supplies. Most of the world's land that is suitable for cultivation is already in use (11 per cent for growing arable crops, 24 per cent for grazing animals), and if a further 4 per cent is utilized by the year 2000 a comparable area could be lost by soil degradation and desertification arising from improper management and climatic conditions. In developed countries increases in yield resulting from greater fertilizer usage are subject to the law of diminishing returns, as seen in the US corn belt where there is a 6 to 10 tonne increase for each tonne of fertilizer added today, compared to 15 to 20 tonne increases about 20 years ago (Brown 1988). The picture is further aggravated by the energy-intensive characteristics of modern agriculture, with substantial consumption being incurred by the chemical production of fertilizers, pesticides, herbicides, and fungicides (greater than 30 per cent of total energy required for agriculture) together with the cost of field operations (about 20 per cent). The need for new thinking about how to achieve food security is obvious. The generic technologies of genetic engineering have been promoted as a means to improve the quality and sustainability of agricultural production in more-developed countries, and output in the less-developed (Beck and Ulrich 1993). Critics of the apparent lack of progress are highly articulate but the demands of high-quality research matched by the regulatory standards for the release of genetically manipulated organisms mitigate against rapid applications. The same critics would not wish it to be otherwise.

Selected examples of current research illustrate options for the establishment of more sustainable systems of food production. Genetic engineering has the potential to reduce the impact of chemicals on the environment, to improve the efficiency of utilization of scarce resources, to reduce waste and spoilage of existing food supplies, and to enhance product quality. Before examining how we should handle these opportunities, it is necessary to review briefly the range of options under consideration.

First, genetically engineered disease resistance in plants and animals has a strong appeal (Broglie and Broglie 1993). Antibody-mediated viral resistance in plants represents a novel application of genetic engineering. Expression of complete or engineered antibodies in plants has recently been achieved and the incidence of artichoke mottled crinkle virus infection has been reduced (Tavladoraki *et al.* 1993). In chickens the introduction of a modified DNA copy of the avian leukosis virus (ALV) illustrates the potential of pathogen-derived resistance as a method for protecting against the normal disease process (Crittenden and Salter 1990). Livestock diseases are a source of serious deprivation and hardship for animals and those who depend on them. In the mid-1980s, it was estimated that pathogens and parasites killed more than 50 million buffaloes and cattle each year, and more than 100 million sheep and goats. Disease was also the cause of a marked reduction in meat quality from these animals. Rapid diagnostic tests have been developed using biotechnological reagents, many produced by genetic engineering

Table 3.1 Selected examples of studies that could lead to a reduced dependence on chemicals

Objective	Genetic modification	Source
Viral protection (plants)	Coat protein-mediated protection Single-chain antibody expression	Beachy *et al.* (1990)
Acquired pesticide (plants)	*Bacillus thuringiensis* insect control protein	Perlak *et al.* (1990)
Insect resistance (plants) Fungal resistance (plants)	Phytoalexins	Braun *et al.* (1991)
Systemic acquired resistance (plants)	Chitinase expression	Broglie and Broglie (1993)
Pathogen-derived resistance (chickens)	Avian leukosis virus	Crittenden and Salter (1990)
Genetically inherited resistance (animals)	Immunoglobulin expression (mouse into mice, pigs, and sheep)	Lo *et al.* (1991)

techniques (OECD 1992). The development of safe, efficient, and less costly vaccines against livestock diseases using recombinant DNA techniques would also have important economic consequences (Munn 1993). In the case of foot-and-mouth disease it could allow developing countries to export their products to countries unaffected by the disease provided that herds were systematically vaccinated with a completely safe, very stable, and easy to produce vaccine (Sasson 1990). The difficulty and complexity of reaching that goal, however, should not be underestimated.

Reduced dependence on chemical usage (Table 3.1) is a long-term objective of improved nitrate utilization and nitrogen fixation, two of the most essential of the natural global processes. Approximately 170 million tonnes of atmospheric nitrogen are converted into ammonia every year, of which 120 million tonnes are attributed to symbiotic nitrogen-fixing microbes. Molecules secreted by rhizobial microbes induce the initial stages of nodulation on the roots of legumes where symbiotic nitrogen fixation occurs. One of these molecules has so far been identified together with the genes of rhizobium which are activated and result in nitrogen fixation for the plant's benefit. Experiments in progress aim to enhance symbiotic nitrogen fixation and induce nodule-like structures on non-legumes such as rice, wheat, and oilseed rape. This would extend the range of species with intrinsic fixation mechanisms and have important repercussions in respect of reduced fertilizer requirements. The technological difficulties for both components of nitrogen utilization are formidable and no one is optimistic that these objectives will be realized in the short term (de Bruijn and Downie 1991).

Secondly, reduced inputs have become a major objective, especially in developed countries where improvement in the efficiency of food production is a high priority. Animal feed is a valuable resource and greater efficiency in protein accretion by livestock would not only improve their value but also conserve inputs of expensive animal, plant, and fish protein (OECD 1992). Growth hormone (GH) is the nearest equivalent to 'nitrogen fixation' in the animal kingdom since it increases the efficiency and improves the quality of protein production (Baumann 1990). The biosynthesis of GH by recombinant DNA technology has resulted in the application of bovine somatotrophin (bST) which causes a significant increase in milk production of 10 to 25 per cent for as long as treatment continues. Lactating Murrah buffalo in India also show an average increase in milk yield of 13 to 24 per cent when treated with bST for 14 days. Improved efficiency of milk production by enhanced utilization of dietary nutrients means that fewer animals would be required in order to produce the same volume of milk, with additional savings from the reduced environmental impact of animal waste. The use of bST in dairy cows farmed under different husbandry conditions, and in different breeds, in various developing countries, including Brazil, Mexico, and Zimbabwe, shows its potential value in less-developed countries. The effects are not confined to lactating cows, since porcine somatotrophin reduces body fat, enhances feed efficiency, and improves protein deposition, at least in the short to medium term, during the active growth phase. Demands for more sustainable systems of livestock production will also be met by improving the time-honoured success of ruminants in the utilization of cellulose in their diet, not only to facilitate the use of lowland and hill pastures but also the digestion of low-quality roughage in animal feed.

Thirdly, reduced waste is currently addressed in some centres by biological treatments involving various forms of vegetation, including water hyacinth, to treat agro-industrial waste and livestock effluent, the hyacinth being recycled for animal feed (Conway and

Pretty 1991). In the poultry industry, arabinoxylans and β-glucans contained in cereal-based diets are not digested in the small intestine and form gel-like and highly viscous structures that are deleterious in terms of nutrition, health, and pollution. Naturally occurring enzymes (xylanases and β-glucanases) are added as supplements, but the enzymes are usually present in complex mixtures. Recombinant DNA technologies have paved the way to isolate and manipulate the genes coding for these enzymes, to produce them in large quantities, and to make enzymes with superior qualities (Coughlan and Hazlewood 1993*a*). A similar approach is being used to improve the cellulose-digesting ability of bacteria which are commonly used in commercial silage inoculants. This improves the consistency of quality and degradability, and diminishes waste (Couglan and Hazlewood 1993*b*).

Finally, the prospect of transferring genes both within and between different species of the same, or different, kingdoms could result in product diversification and enhance competitiveness by improving the value of plant and animal outputs (Table 3.2). Molecular biology provides the means for combining genes derived from distant relatives and unrelated species, and adds to the already vast diversity of organisms. Wild species are sources of evolved resistance and undiscovered pharmaceutical value, so that the future importance of gene banks will become even more significant as genetic engineering is used to provide a friendlier form of food security. Of 250 000 known plant species, fewer than 150 are commercially significant crops and one-tenth of these produce 90 per cent of the world's food energy. The range of genetic diversity among arthropods and micro-organisms, which are more numerous, is even less well explored than among the larger organisms. The provision of new fuels, fibres, construction materials, pharmaceuticals, and chemical feedstuffs for manufacturing industries is already under investigation (Table 3.2), but making greater direct use of the sun, which is the major external energy source available, through photosynthesis has to be one of the most attractive options provided by genetic engineering as a route to the more efficient use of non-renewable resources (Blundell 1993).

The question is whether time is running out because the inherent rate of population growth and the highly regulated technologies of genetic engineering are out of step. Once a gene is successfully transferred and expressed, conventional methods of growing the plants or breeding the animals must be used to evaluate the trait. Clonal propagation in plants and advanced reproductive technologies in livestock (Heap and Moor 1994) mean that the time taken

Table 3.2 Examples of genetic modifications in plants and animals which take advantage of biosynthetic processes to produce high-value compounds

Objective	Genetic modification	Reference
High-value pharmaceuticals	Leu-enkephalin produced in seeds of oilseed rape	Krebbers and Vanderkerckhove (1990)
	Human serum albumin and antibody genes in potato and tobacco plants	Willmitzer and Töpfer (1992)
	Human α_1-antitrypsin in milk of mice and sheep	Archibald *et al.* (1990) Wright *et al.* (1991)
	Human urokinase secreted into mouse milk	Meade *et al.* (1990)
	Heterologous whey acid protein expressed in sow mammary gland	Wall *et al.* (1991)
	Human plasminogen activator in goat milk	Ebert *et al.* (1991)
Improved growth performance in animals	Expression of growth-related peptides in sheep	Rexroad *et al.* (1991)
Improved fibre production in animals	Bacterial genes to improve biosynthesis of cysteine in sheep	Ward (1991)
Designer oils in plants for non-polluting lubricants and food industry	Rape seed oil	Willmitzer and Töpfer (1992)
Detergent synthesis and specialized nutritional requirements	Medium-chain thioesterase expression in oilseed plants	Voelker *et al.* (1992)

Table 3.2 *continued*

Objective	Genetic modification	Reference
Novel oils	Stearoyl-acyl carrier protein desaturase gene in brassica seed oil	Knutzon *et al.* (1992)
Novel polymers	Multistep pathway from a bacterium produces a biodegradable plastic in plants	Poirier *et al.* (1992)
Protection against water stress	Bacterial gene for mannitol-1-phosphate dehydrogenase in tobacco plants	Tarczynski *et al.* (1992)
Production of carbohydrates	Bacterial gene for ADP-glucose phosphorylase increased starch accumulation in potato tubers	Kishore and Somerville (1993)
Modify amino acids in plants for human food and animal feed	Brazil nut 2S albumin gene increased methionine in seeds of tobacco plants	Altenbach *et al.* (1990)
	Increased lysine synthesis after transfer of bacterial enzyme into tobacco plants	Shaul and Galili (1992)

to complete large-scale genetic selection and to disseminate superior stock can be greatly reduced. Yet, as with contraceptive research, the total time from the initial discovery to the satisfactory completion of regulatory issues leading to widespread adoption may still be up to 10 years, or even longer. If the present rate of increase in world population is maintained and food security is unresolved, the crunch will come early in the twenty-first century (Parkes 1993).

MANDATORY CONSTRAINTS

The discoveries of the laws of heredity by Gregor Mendel in the nineteenth century were initially unrecognized, whereas the unravelling of the genetic code by Watson and Crick in the 1950s was hailed internationally. The development of gene splicing techniques in the 1970s for transporting foreign genes into bacteria culminated in an intensive self-imposed and public examination by scientific leaders of the day. This latter discovery, which led to techniques that allow the controlled rearrangement of life's basic substance, provoked fundamental concerns about the impact of biological research on our civilization. It resulted in The Recombinant DNA Research and Development Notification Act of 1980 (USA) which required all persons conducting recombinant DNA research not funded by the National Institutes of Health to file notification of their activities. Local, state, national, and international participation in the regulation of genetic engineering became of paramount importance and, as a direct consequence, regulatory approval has become a critical step in the path of product development and is almost as important as the scientific achievement itself (see Krimsky 1985). Whereas the scientific success achieved in the production of a dazzling array of genetically modified plants and animals could provide agricultural, environmental, and consumer benefits, issues of public perception, public acceptability, and the assessment of need are ignored at our peril. Recent surveys of the public understanding of genetic engineering forewarn of difficulties in the acceptance of products destined for the human food chain. In the EC, a poll of 13 000 voters indicated that the application of genetic engineering to plants and microbes is more acceptable than to livestock. In the US, where public attitudes are more supportive of science and technology, 66 per cent believe that genetic engineering would make life better for people and 82 per cent feel that it should be continued (Office of Technology Assessment 1987). The availability of pharmaceuticals produced by recombinant DNA technology (human insulin for diabetes, human growth hormone for dwarfism, tissue plasminogen activator for heart-attack victims, vaccination against hepatitis B) and successful reports of pulmonary gene therapy in laboratory animals with cystic fibrosis are persuasive examples of how the benefits of genetic engineering could influence clinical practice and serve to build public confidence.

Genetic engineering is a relatively new science, and the release of genetically manipulated organisms is seen as a risk because it lacks a regulatory track record which is longstanding and well proven. The public's perception of risk is influenced not only by the potential hazard but the 'outrage' factor (Sandman 1992) which stems from the negative experiences of introducing new technologies, and from social and cultural attitudes that such methods are unnatural. The technologies are seen to betray a lack of respect of the holistic nature of organisms, or an absence of concern about risk. Public perception has been influenced by activists who are committed to outlawing the technology for multifarious reasons such as its suspected impact on the environment, food, and animal welfare. Jeremy Rifkin's book *Algeny* (the modern alchemy of genes, Rifkin 1984) claims to be the manifesto of a movement to save Nature and simple decency from the hands of rapacious science. Stephen Jay Gould (1990) refutes Rifkin's position and argues that whereas the issues surrounding genetic engineering are complex, *Algeny* is anti-science, anti-intellectual, and against respect for knowledge. Used humanely he sees benefits in medicine and agriculture from genetic engineering for ordinary people. 'I, for one, would rather campaign for proper use, not abolition' (Gould 1990).

Precepts that surround biotechnology are numerous and the Select Committee on Science and Technology of the House of Lords has recently advised that over-regulation is having a negative effect on business competitiveness. The number of environmental release permits in the USA for genetically manipulated plants increased from 5 in 1987 to 1803 in 1994, exemplifying the accelerating activity in this area. Gaining approval for the application of these products requires agreement from three federal agencies (United States Department of Agriculture, Food and Drug Administration, Environment Protection Agency), and a similarly comprehensive evaluation is expected to apply for the EU. For animals, genetic modifications can be carried out in the UK as a regulated procedure only after the Secretary of State has weighed the adverse effects against the benefits likely to accrue (Animals (Scientific Procedures) Act 1986). To ensure that the outcome of any modification can be regarded as harmless, observations of the whole life span of at least two generations of offspring must be carried out. The study of genetically modified animals involving transgenes is also subject to *Guidelines on Work with Transgenic Animals 1989* prepared by the Advisory Committee on Genetic Manipulation of the Health and Safety Executive. Further welfare issues are subject to the general controls of the Protection of Animals Act 1911, and the Agricultural (Miscellaneous Provisions) Act 1968, and the government is advised on farm animal welfare issues by the Farm Animal Welfare Council. Among the controls placed on the use of genetic modification in order to safeguard human health and the environment are included The Genetically

Modified Organisms (Contained Use and Deliberate Release) Regulations of 1992 and 1993.

The food use of such products is controlled under voluntary arrangements administered by two government departments and is due to be superseded by statutory controls introduced under an EC Regulation on Novel Foods. A study group set up by the government to examine the ethics of genetic modification and food use reported in 1993 that they could see no overriding ethical objection which would require the absolute prohibition of the use of organisms containing copy genes of human (or non-human) origin, provided the necessary safety assessment has been fulfilled. This recommendation was posited on the infinitesimal (non-existent) quantity of the original gene in the transformed product. Recognizing the ethical concerns of many groups or individuals who object to the consumption of food containing copy genes of human origin, or from species which are the subject of dietary restrictions for their religion, or of animal origin in the case of vegetarians, it recommended that appropriate food products should be labelled to allow consumers to exercise choice. Two advisory committees assist the government on aspects of work involving the genetic modification of food, and on all aspects of human and environmental health and safety concerning the introduction of genetically manipulated organisms into the UK environment.

Clearly, the provision of regulatory mechanisms is desirable but their profusion can be a powerful disincentive for the constructive use of this relatively new science. The politics surrounding the introduction of genetically engineered bST (bovine somatotrophin) have resulted in a 1 year, followed by a threatened 7 year, moratorium in Europe, although acceptance has just been announced in the USA. As one of the first biotechnology products for food production, bST has the capability of increasing the efficiency of milk production by cattle of both more- and less-developed countries, but has been the topic of intense vilification, mainly on the unproven grounds of product contamination with bST. Concerns also exist about animal welfare associated with repeated treatment, and marginal increases in mastitis, and about its socio-economic impact on small farmers who might be forced out of business. The proposed moratorium will be a disincentive to bringing biotechnology products to the market and it will inhibit potential applications in less-developed countries where the need is great.

Agricultural biotechnology is a market estimated to be worth about £200 million in 1990, with the potential to double or even quadruple in size by 1995 (Table 3.3). These estimates need to be

Table 3.3 Potential markets for biotechnology products, £m (County NatWest WoodMac; Anon 1991)

Market	1990	Optimistic 1995	Pessimistic 1995
Biopesticides			
Bioherbicides	–	16	7
Biofungicides	–	10	–
Bioinsecticides	80	170	110
Total	80	196	117
Seeds			
Herbicide-tolerant	–	200	67
Insect-resistant	–	200	57
Total	–	400	124
Animal health			
Gene-engineered			
vaccines	97	213	120
Diagnostics	17	50	40
Total	114	263	160
Grand total	194	859	401

kept in perspective since the most optimistic forecasts of biotechnology product sales (about £1 billion in 1995) would mean that such products accounted for a very small percentage of the amount spent by farmers on agricultural inputs (3 per cent of global animal health products; 3 per cent of plant seeds with herbicide tolerance or insect resistance; 1 per cent of biopesticides). Much of the research and development has been done by the private sector and it has resulted in chemical companies developing crops resistant to herbicides, which promote the sale of herbicides rather than reduce the use of chemicals in the environment. There is now an active public sector debate about the areas of greatest need, and research is focused increasingly on methods which will reduce inputs, provide chemical alternatives, and improve the effectiveness of sustainable systems.

The desirability of using genetic engineering has so far been considered primarily from its utilitarian or consequential value, but this is a moral theory that is limited because the grounds of right action are not wholly justifiable by the production of good consequences. The question now asked is whether these advances are desirable on the basis of being right, not because of their consequences, but because of natural laws known by human reason, intuition, common sense, or by insights derived from religious traditions (Beauchamp and Childress 1989). Deontology promotes the idea that some intrinsic principles are binding and utility does not of itself permit the adoption of genetic engineering techniques. We have noted previously that such techniques offer the potential to increase the quantity, quality, and safety of food supplies, often by overcoming geographical and climatic obstacles, by the rapid dissemination of disease resistance, and by the widespread distribution of superior genetic qualities compatible with sustainable practices. These advances should not be viewed in isolation since they would require parallel improvements in other disciplines if their application is to be effective. As options they would seem to occupy the moral high ground, provided the techniques adopted are fair for the environment, for animals, and for farmers who have greatest need of their application. Straughan (1989) has discussed the role of modern breeding companies that make use of genetic engineering advances and argues that commercial, legal, and political decision-makers need to show sensitivity 'to a wide range of interests, particularly if those most affected are likely to be the poorest, least influential and most vulnerable individuals'. Funding schemes have been proposed to enable these advances to be applied in developing countries and these are discussed by Persley (1990).

Objectors to the use of genetic engineering include some who identify a 'moral taint' because, for example, the use of animal experimentation to determine the utility of these applications in livestock production makes them ethically unacceptable. Others are concerned with the apparent unnaturalness of the procedures, and with the perception of 'tampering with Nature', even though this has been an activity indulged by humankind in animal and plant selection over many generations. Yet others are concerned about the 'slippery slope' argument. Williams (1985) distinguishes between the *horrible result* argument which objects to what is at the bottom of the slope, and the *arbitrary result* argument which objects to the fact that it is a slope and that there is no simple way to get off. Genetic engineering is perceived by some as being on the 'slippery slope' because it is a short step from the application of these procedures to humans. To many this would personify the *horrible result* argument and is the basis of extant proscriptive legislation. The dilemma that periodically confronts life scientists seeking to answer fundamental questions about development, growth, and differentiation by genetic engineering, and those who use this knowledge to explore options for human fertility regulation or food security is encapsulated in the *arbitrary result* argument. Resolving that dilemma depends on the exercise of individual choice and the gaining of public acceptability. For both parties ethical issues have become increasingly prominent.

Adopting biotechnology may offer future options for escaping the Malthusian trap which, put simply, postulates that the universal tendency for the population of a country to grow at a geometric rate with food supplies expanding at a roughly arithmetic rate results in poor nations that are unable to rise above their subsistence level per capita income unless they check their population growth. In the absence of preventive checks such as pregnancy spacing, positive checks will inevitably occur (starvation, disease, wars). Malthusian and neo-Malthusian theories, however, have largely failed to take adequate account of the role and impact of technological progress, and the complex individual factors that determine family size (Todaro 1989). The danger for those who promote biotechnology is the emerging techno-mythology which encourages the simplistic belief that we can fine-tune Nature and preserve its diversity while reaping its bounty. Krimsky (1994) sees such myths as hopeful symbols, as speculations, exaggerations, or even false notions of hope, but designed to achieve social commitment to a unanimity of purpose. Techno-myths surface repeatedly in the journalism of today and the gene is given almost a metaphysical status based on flawed science that discounts the environmental context in which we and our genes exist (Hubbard and Wald 1993). Krimsky (1994) predicts that the strongest effort at mythmaking for biotechnology is to be expected when there is the greatest threat of commercialization of its products, an assessment well illustrated in recent issues reported in the quality press.

Finally, this brings us to consider whether the Biorevolution is really another form of the Green Revolution? The Biorevolution forms a major part of the modern technological advance and, in contradistinction to the former Green Revolution, its potential impact is likely to be more comprehensive since it is confined neither to crop production nor to a dependency on a continuous level of expensive inputs. The social opposition which has arisen to the new technologies encompasses issues of social justice and environmental concerns, the extent to which research and development is becoming increasingly the responsibility of the private rather than public sector, and the movement from nationally ordered to internationally marketed high-value products aimed at affluent consumers. All these components are relevant to the future and did not apply to the Green Revolution (Buttel 1994). Whereas the future is difficult to predict, Dennis Gabor, Nobel laureate and the inventor of holography, wrote that futures can be invented. We are faced with inventing a future that includes genetic engineering which could enlarge the options for the spacing of pregnancy, for enhanced food security, and for reduced environmental damage. The difficult question is, what kind of future is worth inventing, and how should we regulate it?

REFERENCES

Aitken, R. J., Paterson, M., and Thillai Koothan, P. (1993). Contraceptive vaccines. In *Contraception* (ed. J. O. Drife and D. T. Baird). *British Medical Bulletin*, **49**, 88–99.

Altenbach, S., Person, K., Meeker, G., Staraci, L., and Sun, S. (1990). Enhancement of the methionine content of seed proteins by the expression of a chimeric gene encoding a methionine rich protein in transgenic plants. *Plant Molecular Biology*, **13**, 513–22.

Anon (1991). Potential markets for biotechnological products (County NatWest WoodMac). *Biotechnology Business News*, **1**, (18), 10.

Archibald, A. L., McClenaghan, M., Hornsey, V., Simons, J. P., and Clark, A.J. (1990). High-level expression of biologically active human α_1-antitrypsin in the milk of transgenic mice. *Proceedings of the National Academy of Sciences USA*, **87**, 5178–82.

Arevalo, J. H., Stura, E. A., Taussig, M. J., and Wilson, I. A. (1993). Three dimensional structure of an anti-steroid fab′ and progesterone-fab′ complex. *Journal of Molecular Biology*, **231**, 103–18.

Baird, D. T. (1993) Antigestogens. In *Contraception* (ed. J. O. Drife and D. T. Baird). *British Medical Bulletin*, **49**, 73–87.

Baumann, D. E. (1990). *Bovine somatotrophin: review of an emerging animal technology.* Office of Technology Assessment, Congress of the United States, Washington DC.

Beachy, R. N., Loesch-Fries, S., and Tumer N. E. (1990). Coat protein-mediated resistance against virus infection. *Annual Review of Phytopathology*, **28**, 451–74.

Beauchamp, T. L. and Childress, J. F. (1989). *Principles of biomedical ethics*. Cambridge University Press.

Beck, C. I. and Ulrich, T. (1993). Biotechnology in the food industry. *Biotechnology*, **11**, 895–902.

Blobel, C. P., Wolfsberg, T. G., Turck, C. W., Myles, D. G., Primakoff, P., and White, J. M. (1992). A potential fusion peptide and an integrin ligand domain in a protein active in sperm-egg fusion. *Nature*, **356**, 248–52.

Blundell, T. L. (1993). The benefits of biotechnology to agriculture and other biology based industries. *Proceedings 'Biotechnology, Friend or Foe'*, ed. D. J. Bennett.

Braun, C. J., Jilka, J. M., Hemenway, C. L., and Turner, N. E. (1991). Interactions between plants, pathogens and insects: possibilities for engineering resistance. *Current Opinion in Biotechnology*, **2**, 193–8.

Broglie, R. and Broglie, K. (1993). Production of disease-resistant transgenic plants. *Current Opinion in Biotechnology*, **4**, 148–51.

Brown, D. and Rothery, P. (1993). *Models in biology: mathematics, statistics and computing*. Wiley, Sussex.

Brown, L. R. (1988). The growing Grain Gap. *Worldwatch*, Sept.–Oct., pp. 32–40.

Brundtland, G. E. (1989). How to secure our common future. *Scientific American*, **261**, 134.

Buttel, F. H. (1994). Global impacts of agricultural biotechnology: a post-green revolution perspective. In *Issues in agricultural bioethics*. University of Nottingham Press (in press).

Conway, G. R. and Pretty, J. N. (1991). *Unwelcome harvest; agriculture and pollution*. Earthscan Publications, London.

Coughlan, M. P. and Hazlewood, G. P. (1993a). β-1,4-D-xylan-degrading enzyme systems: biochemistry, molecular biology and applications. *Biotechnology and Applied Biochemistry*, 17, 259–89.

Coughlan, M. P. and Hazlewood, G. P. (1993b). *Hemicellulose and hemicellulases*. Portland Press, London.

Crittenden, L. B. and Salter, D. W. (1990). Transgenic chickens resistant to avian leukosis virus. In *Proceedings of the 4th World Congress on Genetics Applied to Livestock Production, Edinburgh, 23–27 July 1990*, pp. 453–6.

Daily, G. C., Ehrlich, A. H., and Ehrlich, P. R. (1993). Optimum human population size. *First World Optimim Population Congress, Cambridge* (in press).

de Bruijn, F. J. and Downie, J. A. (1991). Biochemical and molecular studies of symbiotic nitrogen fixation. *Current Opinion in Biotechnology*, 2, 184–92.

Djerassi, C. (1992). *The pill, pygmy chimps and Degas horse*. Basic Books, New York.

Drife, J. O. and Baird, D. T. (1993). Contraception. *British Medical Bulletin*, 49, 1–258.

Ebert, K. M., *et al.* (1991). Transgenic production of a variate of human tissue-type plasminogen activator in goat milk: generation of transgenic goats and analysis of expression. *Biotechnology*, 9, 835–8.

Garnett, G. P. and Anderson, R. M. (1993). No reason for complacency about the potential demographic impact of AIDS in Africa. *Transactions of the Royal Society of Tropical Medicine and Hygiene*, 87, (Suppl. 1), 19–22.

Gould, S. J. (1990). Integrity and Mr Rifkin. In *An urchin in the storm*. Penguin, London.

Hardin, G. (1993). *Living within limits*. Oxford University Press, New York.

Heap, R. B. and Moor, R. M. (1994). Reproductive technologies in farm animals: ethical issues. *Issues in agricultural bioethics*. Nottingham University Press (in press).

Heap, R. B., Taussig, M. J., Wang, M.-W., and Whyte, A. (1992). Antibodies, implantation and embryo survival. *Reproduction, Fertilization, Development*, 4, 467–80.

Hubbard, R. and Wald, E. (1993). *Exploding the gene myth*. Beacon Press, Boston.

Jones, R., Shalgi, R., Hoyland, J., and Phillips, D.M. (1993). Topographical rearrangement of a plasma membrane antigen during capacitation of rat spermatozoa *in vitro*. *Developmental Biology*, 139, 349–63.

King, I. and Slessor, M. (1993). Prospects for sustainable development: the significance of population growth. *First World Optimum Population Congress, Cambridge* (in press).

Kishore, G. M. and Somerville, C. R. (1993). Genetic engineering of commercially useful biosynthetic pathways in transgenic plants. *Current Opinion in Biotechnology*, **4**, 152–8.

Knutzon, D. S., Thompson, G. A., Radke, S. E., Johnson, W. B., Knauf, V. C., and Kridl, J. C. (1992). Modification of brassica seed oil by antisense expression of a stearoyltacyl carrier protein desaturase gene. *Proceedings of the National Academy of Sciences USA*, **89**, 2524–628.

Krebbers, E. and Vandekerckhove, J. (1990). Production of peptides in plant seeds. *Trends in Biotechnology*, **8**, 1–3.

Krimsky, S. (1985). *Genetic alchemy: the social history of the recombinant DNA controversy*. MIT Press, Cambridge, Massachusetts.

Krimsky, S. (1994). The cultural and symbolic dimensions of agricultural biotechnology. In *Issues in agricultural bioethics*. Nottingham University Press (in press).

Kupchella, C. E. and Hyland, M. C. (1986). *Environmental science. Living within the system of nature*. Prentice-Hall, USA.

Lincoln, D. W. (1993). Contraception for the year 2020. In *Contraception* (ed. J. O. Drife and D. T. Baird). *British Medical Bulletin*, **49**, 222–36.

Lo, D., *et al.* (1991). Expression of mouse IgA by transgenic mice, pigs and sheep. *European Journal of Immunology*, **21**, 1001–6.

Malthus, T. (1798). *An essay on the principle of population and a summary view of the principle of population*, (ed. A. Flew). Penguin Classics, GB.

Mann, J., Tarantola, D. J. M., and Netter, T. W. (1992). *AIDS in the World*. Harvard University Press, Cambridge, Massachusetts.

Meade, H., Gates, L., Lacy, E., and Lonberg, N. (1990). Bovine αs1-casein gene sequences direct high level expression of active human urokinase in mouse milk. *Biotechnology*, **8**, 443–6.

Munn, E. A. (1993). Development of a vaccine against *Haemonchus contortus*. *Parasitology Today*, **9**, 338–9.

OECD (1992). Biotechnology, Agriculture and Food, Paris.

OTA (1987). *New developments in biotechnology, background paper: public perceptions of biotechnology*. US Government Printing Office, Washington DC.

Parkes, A. S. (1993). *Backlash; a biologist looks at the problems of population and the environment*. Cambridge University Press, Cambridge.

Perlak, F. J., *et al.* (1990). Insect resistant cotton plants. *Biotechnology*, **8**, 939–43.

Persley, G. J. (1990). *Agricultural biotechnology; opportunities for international development*. CAB International, Wallingford.

Pimentel, M. (1989). Food as a resource. In *Food and natural resources* (ed. D. Pimentel and C. W. Hall). Academic Press, London.

Poirier, Y. P., Dennis, D. E., Klomparens, K., and Somerville, C. R. (1992). Production of polyhydroxybutyrate, a biodegradable thermoplastic, in higher plants. *Science*, **256**, 520–3.

Potts, D. M. and Crane, S. F. (1993). Contraceptive delivery in the developing world. *British Medical Bulletin*, **49**, 27–39.

Raghupathy, R. and Talwar, G. P. (1992). Vaccines against fertility. *Current Opinion in Immunology*, **4**, 597–602.

Rexroad, C. E. Jnr, *et al.* (1991). Transferrin- and albumin-directed expression of growth-related peptides in transgenic sheep. *Journal of Animal Science*, **69**, 2995–3004.

Richardson, D., Evans, R., Sayigh, A. A., and Kinzett S. (1993). The optimum population of the United Kingdom. In *First World Optimum Population Congress, Cambridge* (in press).

Rifkin, J. (1984). *Algeny—a new word, a new world*. Penguin, London.

Sandman, P. M. (1992). Hazard versus outrage. *IOMA Broadcaster*, 6–17.

Sasson, A. (1990). *Feeding tomorrow's world*. Unesco, Paris.

Shaul, O. and Galili, G. (1992). Increased lysine synthesis in tobacco plants that express high levels of bacterial dihydrodipicolinate synthase in their chloroplasts. *Plant Journal*, **2**, 203–9.

Simon, J. and Kahn, H. (1984). *The resourceful Earth*. Blackwell, Oxford.

Sinclair, A. R. E. (1990). Population regulation in animals. In *Ecological concepts: the contribution of ecology to an understanding of the natural world* (ed. J. M. Cherrett *et al.*), pp. 197–241. Blackwell Scientific Publications, Oxford.

Straughan, R. (1989). *The genetic manipulation of plants, animals and microbes. The social and ethical issues for consumers: a discussion*. National Consumer Council, 20 Grosvenor Gardens, London.

Talwar, G. P., *et al.* (1993). A birth control vaccine is on the horizon for family planning. *Annals of Medicine*, **25**, 207–12.

Tarczynski, M. C., Jensen, R. G., and Bohnert, H. J. (1992). Stress protection of transgenic tobacco by production of the osmolyte mannitol. *Science*, **259**, 508–10.

Tavladoraki, P., Benvenuto, E., Trinca, S., De Martinis, D., Cattaneo, A., and Galeffi, P. (1993). Transgenic plants expressing a functional single-chain Fv antibody are specifically protected from virus attack. *Nature*, **366**, 469–72.

Thorogood, M. and Villard-Mackintosh, L. (1993). Combined oral contraceptives: risks and benefits. In *Contraception* (ed. J. O. Drife and D. T. Baird). *British Medical Bulletin*, **49**, 124–39.

Todaro, M. P. (1989). *Economic development in the Third World*. Longman, New York.

Voelker, T. A., *et al.* (1992). Fatty acid biosynthesis redirected to medium chains in transgenic oilseed plants. *Science*, **257**, 72–4.

Wall, R. J., Pursel, V. G., Shamay, A., McKnight, R. A., Pittius C. W., and Hennighausen, L. (1991). High-level synthesis of a heterologous milk protein in the mammary glands of transgenic swine. *Proceedings of the National Academy of Sciences USA*, **8**, 1696–700.

Wang, M.-W. and Heap, R. B. (1992). Vaccination against pregnancy. In *Oxford Reviews of Reproductive Biology* (ed. S. R. Milligan), Vol. 14, pp. 101–40. Oxford University Press, Oxford.

Ward, K. A. (1991). The application of transgenic techniques for the improvement of domestic animal productivity. *Current Opinion in Biotechnology*, **2**, 834–9.

Whitehead, R. (1991). Famine. In *The fragile environment*, The Darwin College Lectures (ed. L. Friday and R. Laskey), pp. 82–106. Cambridge University Press, Cambridge.

Williams, B. (1985). Which slopes are slippery? In *Modern dilemmas in modern medicine* (ed. M. Lockwood), pp. 126–37. Oxford University Press, Oxford.

Willmitzer, L. and Töpfer, R. (1992). Manipulation of oil, starch and protein composition. *Current Opinion in Biotechnology*, **3**, 176–80.

World Commission on Environment and Development (1987). *Our Common Future*. Oxford University Press, Oxford.

Wright, G., *et al.* (1991). High level expression of active human alpha-1-antitrypsin in the milk of transgenic sheep. *Biotechnology*, **9**, 830–4.

4

The potential effects of climate change on world food supply

Martin Parry

After graduating at the University of Durham and taking a Master's degree at the University of the West Indies, Professor Parry was awarded his doctorate at the University of Edinburgh in 1973 for research in geography. In the same year he was appointed to a lectureship in geography at the University of Birmingham, where he subsequently held the appointments of Senior Lecturer, Reader in Resource Management and, from 1989, Professor of Environmental Management. In 1991, Martin Parry was appointed to be the first IBM Director of the newly established Environmental Change Unit in the University of Oxford and became a Professorial Fellow of Linacre College. He has held a number of visiting appointments overseas, including that of Director of the Climate Impacts Project at the International Institute for Applied Systems Analysis in Austria. In 1993 Professor Parry was a joint winner of the Norbert Gerbier-Mumm International Award for work in applied meteorology. He left Oxford in 1994 in order to take up the post of Professor of Environmental Management and Director of Environmental Studies at University College, London.

BACKGROUND

This chapter reports the findings of a major study undertaken by the Environmental Change Unit at Oxford, in conjunction with Columbia University in New York City. An additional summary of this work has been published elsewhere (Rosenzweig and Parry 1994). There are two main components to this study: the estimation of potential changes in crop yield, and the estimation of world food trade responses.

Potential changes in national grain crop yields were estimated using crop models and a decision support system developed by the US Agency for International Development's International Benchmark Sites Network for Agrotechnology Transfer (IBSNAT 1989). The crops modelled were wheat, rice, maize, and soybeans. These crops account for more than 85 per cent of the world's traded grains and legumes. The estimated yield changes for the 18 countries were interpolated to provide estimates of yield changes for all regions of the world and for all the major crops, by reference to all available published and unpublished information.

These yield changes were used as inputs into a world food trade model, the Basic Linked System (BLS), developed at the International Institute for Applied Systems Analysis (IIASA) (Fischer *et al.* 1988). Outputs from simulations by the BLS provided information on food production, food prices, and on the number of people at risk from hunger.

Climate change scenarios

Scenarios of climate change were developed in order to estimate their effects on crop yields and food trade. A climate change scenario is defined as a physically consistent set of changes in meteorological variables, based on generally accepted projections of levels of CO_2 (and other trace gases). The range of scenarios used is intended to capture the range of possible effects and to set limits on the associated uncertainty. The scenarios for this study were created by changing observed data on current climate (1951–80) according to doubled CO_2 simulations of three general circulation models (GCMs). The GCMs used are those from the Goddard Institute for Space Studies (GISS), Geophysical Fluid Dynamics Laboratory (GFDL), and United Kingdom Meteorological Office (UKMO). Mean monthly changes in climate variables from the appropriate gridbox were applied to observed daily climate records to create climate change scenarios for each site.

GCMs currently provide the most advanced means of predicting the potential future climatic consequences of increasing radiatively active trace gases. They have been shown to simulate current temperatures reasonably well, but do not reproduce current precipitation as accurately, and their ability to reproduce current climate varies considerably from region to region (Houghton *et al.* 1990). They have not yet been validated to project changes in climate variability, such as changes in the frequencies of drought and storms, even though these could affect crop yields significantly.

Rates of future emissions of trace gases, as well as when the full magnitude of their effects will be realized, are not certain. Because other greenhouse gases besides CO_2 (e.g. methane (CH_4), nitrous oxide (N_2O), and the chlorofluorocarbons (CFCs)) are also increasing, an 'effective CO_2 doubling' has been defined as the combined radiative forcing of all greenhouse gases having the same forcing as doubled CO_2 (usually defined as 600 ppm). For this study, CO_2 concentrations in 2060 are estimated to be 555 ppm (based on

Hansen *et al.* 1988). The effective CO_2 doubling will occur around the year 2030, if current emission trends continue. The climate change caused by an effective doubling of CO_2 may be delayed by 30–40 years or longer, hence the projections for 2060 in this study.

Crop models and yield simulations

Crop models

The IBSNAT crop models were used to estimate how climate change and increasing levels of carbon dioxide may alter yields of world crops at 112 sites, representing both major production areas and vulnerable regions at low, mid, and high latitudes. The IBSNAT models employ simplified functions to predict the growth of crops as influenced by the major factors that affect yields, that is genetics, climate (daily solar radiation, maximum and minimum temperatures, and precipitation), soils, and management practices. Models used were for wheat (Ritchie and Otter 1985; Godwin *et al.* 1989), maize (Jones and Kiniry 1986; Ritchie *et al.* 1989), paddy and upland rice (Godwin *et al.* 1992), and soybean (Jones *et al.* 1989).

The IBSNAT models were selected for use in this study because they have been validated over a wide range of environments (see Otter-Nacke *et al.* 1986) and are not specific to any particular location or soil type. They are thus suitable for use in large-area studies in which crop growing conditions differ greatly. The validation of the crop models over different environments also improves the ability to estimate effects of changes in climate. Furthermore, because management practices such as the choice of varieties, the planting date, fertilizer application, and irrigation may be varied in the models, they permit experiments that simulate adjustments by farmers and agricultural systems to climate change.

Physiological effects of CO_2

Most plants growing in experimental environments with increased levels of atmospheric CO_2 exhibit increased rates of net photosynthesis (i.e. total photosynthesis minus respiration) and reduced stomatal openings. (Experimental effects of CO_2 on crops have been reviewed by Acock and Allen (1985) and Cure (1985).) By so doing, CO_2 reduces transpiration per unit leaf area while enhancing photosynthesis. Thus it often improves water-use efficiency (the ratio of crop biomass accumulation or yield and the amount of water used in evapotranspiration).

The crop models used in this study account for the beneficial physiological effects of increased atmospheric CO_2 concentrations on crop growth and water use (Peart *et al.* 1989). Ratios were calculated between measured daily photosynthesis and evapotranspiration rates for a canopy exposed to high CO_2 values, based on published experimental results (Kimball 1983; Cure and Acock 1986; Allen *et al.* 1987), and the ratios were applied to the appropriate variables in the crop models on a daily basis. The photosynthesis ratios (555 ppm CO_2/330 ppm CO_2) for soybean, wheat and rice, and maize were 1.21, 1.17, and 1.06, respectively. These effects are based on experimental results that may overstate the positive effects of CO_2, because uncertainty exists concerning the extent to which the beneficial effects of increasing CO_2 will be seen in crops growing in variable, windy, and pest-infected (weeds, insects, and diseases) fields under climate change conditions.

Limitations of crop growth models

The crop models embody a number of simplifications. For example, weeds, diseases, and insect pests are assumed to be controlled; there are no problem soil conditions (e.g. high salinity or acidity); and there are no extreme weather events, such as heavy storms. The crop models simulate the current range of agricultural technologies available around the world. They do not include induced improvements in such technology, but may be used to test the effects of some potential improvements, such as the introduction of varieties with higher thermal requirements and installation of irrigation systems.

Yield simulations

Crop modelling simulation experiments were performed at the 112 sites in 18 countries for baseline climate (1951–80) and GCM doubled CO_2 climate change scenarios, with and without the physiological effects of CO_2. This involved the following tasks:

1. The geographical boundaries were defined for the major production regions in the country studies, and the current production of major crops in those regions was estimated.

2. Observed climate data for representative sites within these regions were provided for the baseline period (1951–80), or for as many years of daily data as were available, and the soil, crop variety, and management inputs necessary to run the crop models at the selected sites were specified.

3. The crop models were validated with experimental data from field trials.

4. The crop models were run with baseline data and climate change scenarios, with and without the direct effects of CO_2 on crop growth.

5. Alterations in agricultural practices that would lessen any adverse consequences of climate change, by simulating irrigated production and other adaptation responses (e.g. shifts in planting date and crop varieties) were identified and evaluated.

Deriving estimates of potential yield changes

Aggregation of site results

Crop model results for wheat, rice, maize and soybean from the 112 sites in the 18 countries were aggregated by weighting regional yield changes (based on current production) to estimate changes in national yields. The regional yield estimates represent the current mix of rainfed and irrigated production, the current crop varieties, nitrogen management, and soils. The study simulated 70–75 per cent of the world production of wheat and maize. Even though only two countries (Brazil and USA) simulated soybean production, their combined output accounts for 76 per cent of world total. Less of the total world rice production was simulated than total production of the other crops. This is because India, Indonesia, and Vietnam have significant rice production not included in the study. Production data were gathered by scientists participating in the project and from the FAO (1988), the USDA Crop Production Statistical Division, and the USDA International Service.

Yield change estimates for crops and regions not simulated

Changes in national yields of other crops and commodity groups and regions which were not simulated were estimated on the basis of similarities to modelled crops and growing conditions, previous published and unpublished climate change impact studies, and GCM climate change scenarios. Estimates were made of yield changes for the three GCM scenarios with and without the direct effects of CO_2. The yield changes with the direct effects of CO_2 were based on the mean responses to CO_2 for the different crops in the crop model simulations.

The primary source of uncertainty in the estimates lies in the sparseness of the crop modelling sites. They may not adequately represent the variability of agricultural regions within countries, the variability of agricultural systems within similar agro-ecological zones, or dissimilar agricultural regions. However, since the site results relate to regions that account for about 70 per cent of world grain production, the conclusions concerning world totals of production contained in this report are believed to be adequately substantiated.

The world food trade model

The estimates of climate-induced changes in yields were used as inputs to a dynamic model of the world food system (the Basic Linked System) in order to assess possible impacts on future levels of food production, on food prices, and on the number of people at risk from hunger. Impacts were assessed for the year 2060, with population growth, technology trends, and economic growth projected to that year. Assessments were first made assuming no climate change, and subsequently with the climate change scenarios described above. The difference between the two assessments is the climate-induced effect. A further set of assessments examined the efficacy of a number of adaptations at the farm level in mitigating the impacts and the effect on future production of liberalizing the world food trade system, and of different rates of growth of economy and population.

The Basic Linked System (BLS) consists of linked national models. The BLS was designed at the International Institute for Applied Systems Analysis for food policy studies, but it can also be used to evaluate the effect of climate-induced changes in yield on world food supply and agricultural prices. It consists of 20 national and/or regional models which cover about 80 per cent of the world food system. The remaining 20 per cent is covered by 14 regional models for the countries which have broadly similar attributes (e.g. African oil-exporting countries, Latin American high-income exporting countries, Asian low-income countries, etc.). The grouping is based on country characteristics such as geographical location, income per capita, and the country's position with regard to net food trade.

The BLS is a general equilibrium model system, with representation of all economic sectors, empirically estimated parameters and no unaccounted supply sources or demand sinks (see Fischer *et al.* 1988 for a complete description of the model). In the BLS, countries are linked through trade, world market prices, and financial flows. It is a recursively dynamic system: a first round of exports from all countries is calculated for an assumed set of world prices, and international market clearance is checked for each commodity. World prices are then revised, using an optimizing algorithm and again transmitted to the national model. Next, these generate new domestic equilibria and adjust net exports. This process is repeated until the world markets are cleared in all commodities. At each stage of the reiteration domestic markets are in equilibrium. This process yields international prices as influenced by governmental and intergovernmental agreements.

The system is solved in annual increments, simultaneously for all countries. Summary indicators of the sensitivity of the world system used in this report include world cereal production, world cereal prices, and proportion of world population at risk from hunger (this is defined as the population with an income insufficient to either produce or procure their food requirements).

The BLS does not incorporate any climate relationships *per se*. Effects of changes in climate were introduced to the model as changes in the average national or regional yield per commodity, as estimated above. Ten commodities are included in the model: wheat, rice, coarse grains (maize, millet, sorghum, barley, etc.) bovine and ovine meat, dairy products, other animal products, protein feeds, other food, non-food agriculture, and non-agriculture. In this report, however, consideration is limited to the major grain food crops.

The set of model experiments

The results described in this chapter are for the following scenarios:

The reference scenario

This involved projection of the agricultural system to the year 2060 with no effects of climate change on yields and with no major changes in the political or economic context of the world food trade. It assumes:

- UN medium population estimates, which are 10.2 billion by 2060 (UN 1989; IBRD/World Bank 1990);

- 50 per cent trade liberalization in agriculture introduced gradually by 2020;

- moderate economic growth (ranging from 3.0 per cent per annum in 1980–2000 to 1.1 per cent per annum in 2040–60);

- technology is projected to increase yields over time (cereal yields of world total, developing countries, and developed countries are assumed to increase annually by 0.7 per cent, 0.9 per cent, and 0.6 per cent, respectively);

- no changes in agricultural productivity due to climate change.

The climate change scenarios

These are projections of the world food system including effects on agricultural yields under different climate scenarios (the '2 × CO_2 scenarios' for the GISS, GFDL, and UKMO GCMs). The food trade simulations for these three scenarios were started in 1990 and assumed a linear change in yields until the doubled CO_2 changes are reached in 2060. Simulations were made both with and without the physiological effects of 555 ppm CO_2 on crop growth and yield for the equilibrium yield estimates. In these scenarios internal adjustments in the model occur, such as increased agricultural investment, reallocation of agricultural resources according to economic returns, and reclamation of additional arable land as an adjustment to higher cereal prices, based on shifts in comparative advantage among countries and regions.

Scenarios including the effects of farm-level adaptations

The food trade model was first run with yield changes assuming no external adaptation to climate change and was then re-run with different climate-induced changes in yield assuming a range of farm-level adaptations. These include such measures as switching planting dates, changing crop varieties, and the use of different amounts of irrigation and fertilizer.

Two adaptation levels to cope with potential effects on yield and agriculture were considered. Adaptation level 1 includes those adaptations at the farm level that would not involve any major changes in agricultural practices. It thus included changes in planting date, in amounts of irrigation, and in choice of crop varieties that are currently available. Adaptation level 2 includes, in addition to the former, major changes in agricultural practices, for example large shifts of planting date, the availability of new cultivars, extensive expansion of irrigation, and increased fertilizer application. This level of adaptation would be likely to involve policy changes at the national and international level and would be likely to involve significant costs. However, policy, cost, and water resource availability were not studied explicitly.

Scenarios of different future trade, economic and population growth

A final set of scenarios assumed changes to the world tariff structure and different rates of growth of economy and population. As with the previous experiments, these were conducted both with and without climate change impacts. These scenarios included:

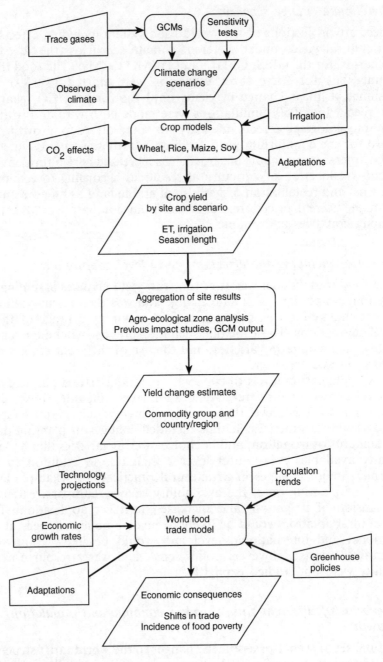

Fig. 4.1 Key elements of the approach.

Table 4.1 Current production and changes in simulated wheat yields under GCM 2 × CO₂ climate change scenarios, with and without the direct effects of CO_2.[a]

Country	Current production			Change in simulated yields					
	Yield (t/ha)	Area (ha × 1000)	Production (t × 1000)	GISS[b] (%)	GFDL[b] (%)	UKMO[b] (%)	GISS[c] (%)	GFDL[c] (%)	UKMO[c] (%)
Australia	1.38	11 546	15 574	−18	−16	−14	−8	11	9
Brazil	1.31	2788	3625	−51	−38	−53	−33	−17	−34
Canada	1.88	11 365	21 412	−12	−10	−38	27	27	−7
China	2.53	29 092	73 527	−5	−12	−17	16	8	0
Egypt	3.79	572	2166	−36	−28	−54	−31	−26	−51
France	5.93	4636	27 485	−12	−28	−23	4	−15	−9
India	1.74	22 876	39 703	−32	−38	−56	3	−9	−33
Japan	3.25	237	772	−18	−21	−40	−1	−5	−27
Pakistan	1.73	7478	12 918	−57	−29	−73	−19	31	−55
Uruguay	2.15	91	195	−41	−48	−50	−23	−31	−35
Former USSR									
winter	2.46	18 988	46 959	−3	−17	−22	29	9	0
spring	1.14	36 647	41 959	−12	−25	−48	21	3	−25
USA	2.72	26 595	64 390	−21	−23	−33	−2	−2	−14
World[d]	2.09	231	482	−16	−22	−33	−11	−4	−13

[a] Results for each country represent the site results weighted according to regional production. The world estimates represent the country results weighted by national production. Source: Rosenzweig and Parry, 1994.
[b] GCM 2 × CO₂ climate change scenario alone.
[c] GCM 2 × CO₂ climate change scenario with direct effects of CO₂.
[d] World area and production ×1 000 000.

- full trade liberalization in agriculture introduced gradually by 2020:
- lower economic growth, ranging from 2.7 per cent per annum in 1980–2000, to 1.0 per cent in 2040–60 (global gross domestic product (GDP) in 2060 is 10.3 per cent lower than the reference scenario, 11.2 per cent lower in developing countries, and 9.8 per cent lower in developed countries);
- low population growth, UN low population estimates (*c.* 8.6 billion by 2060).

EFFECTS ON YIELDS

Yields without adaptation

Table 4.1 shows wheat yield changes by GCM $2 \times CO_2$ climate change scenario for the countries where crop model simulations were conducted. Results show that climate change scenarios without the direct physiological effects of CO_2 cause decreases in simulated crop yields in many cases, while the direct effects of CO_2 mitigate the negative effects primarily in mid and high latitudes.

The magnitudes of the estimated yield changes vary by crop. Maize production is most negatively affected, probably due to its lower response to the physiological effects of CO_2 on crop growth. Protein feed is least affected because soybean responds significantly to increased CO_2, at least under the scenarios of smaller increases in temperature (e.g. the GISS and GFDL scenarios).

The differences between countries in yield responses to climate change are related to differences in current growing conditions. At low latitudes, crops are grown nearer the limits of temperature tolerances and global warming may subject crops to higher stress. In many mid- and high-latitude areas increased temperatures can benefit crops otherwise limited by cold temperatures and short growing seasons in the present climate.

The primary causes of decreases in yield are:

1. Shortening of the growing period (especially grain-filling stage) of the crop. This occurred at some sites in all countries.
2. Decrease of water availability. This is increased by evapotranspiration and loss of soil moisture and in some cases a decrease in precipitation in the climate change scenarios. This occurred in Argentina, Brazil, Canada, France, Japan, Mexico, and the USA.
3. Poor vernalization. Some temperate cereal crops require a

period of low temperature in winter to initiate or accelerate the flowering process. Low vernalization results in low flower bud initiation and ultimately reduced yields. This caused decreases in winter wheat yields at some sites in Canada and the former USSR.

Figure 4.2 shows estimated potential changes in average national crop yields for the GISS, GFDL, and UKMO $2 \times CO_2$ climate change scenarios allowing for the direct effects of CO_2 on plant growth. Latitudinal differences are apparent in all the scenarios. High latitude changes are less negative or even positive in some cases, while lower latitude regions indicate more detrimental effects of climate change on agricultural yields.

The GISS and GFDL climate change scenarios produced yield changes ranging from +30 per cent to −30 per cent. The GISS scenario is, in general, more detrimental than GFDL to crop yields in parts of Asia and South America, while GFDL results in more negative yields in the USA and Africa and less positive results in the former USSR. The UKMO climate change scenario, which has the greatest warming (5.2 °C global surface air temperature increase), causes yield declines almost everywhere (up to 50 per cent in Pakistan).

Yields with adaptation

The study tested the efficacy of two levels of adaptation. Level 1 implies little change to existing agricultural systems, reflecting farmer response to a changing climate. Level 2 implies more substantial change to agricultural systems, possibly requiring resources beyond the farmer's means. Level 2 adaptation represents an optimistic assessment of world agriculture's response to changed climate conditions as predicted by the GCMs tested in this study. In each case, the adaptations were tested as possible responses to the worst climate change scenario (this was usually, but not always, the UKMO scenario). Changes in economic or domestic agricultural policies were beyond the scope of this study; the costs of adaptation and future water availability under the climate change scenarios were also not considered.

Level 1 adaptation includes:

1. shifts in planting date that do not imply major changes in crop calendar;
2. additional application of irrigation water to crops already under irrigation; and

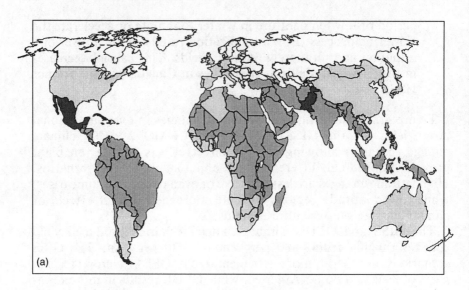

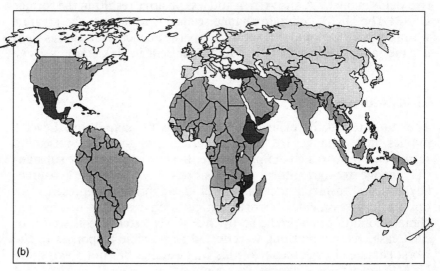

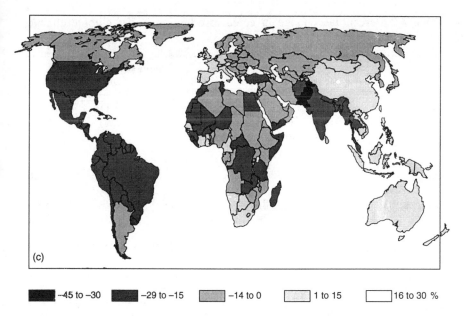

-45 to -30   -29 to -15   -14 to 0   1 to 15   16 to 30 %

Fig. 4.2 Change in crop yields under the three climate change scenarios, with the direct effects of CO_2. (a) GISS $2 \times CO_2$; (b) GFDL $2 \times CO_2$; (c) UKMO $2 \times CO_2$.

3. changes in crop variety to currently available varieties more adapted to the projected climate.

Level 2 adaptation includes:

1. large shifts in planting date;
2. increased fertilizer application;
3. development of new varieties; and
4. installation of irrigation systems.

Yield changes for both adaptation levels were based on crop model simulations where available, and were extended to other crops and regions using the estimation methods described above. The adaptation estimates were developed only for the scenarios with the direct effects of CO_2 as these were judged to be most realistic.

Table 4.2 Percentage change in cereal production under climate change scenarios in 2060

Region	Reference scenario (2060) without climate change (mmt)[a]	Scenario with climate change		
		GISS (%)	GFDL (%)	UKMO (%)
Global	3286	−1.2	−2.8	−7.6
Developed	1449	11.3	5.2	−3.5
Developing	1836	−11.0	−9.2	−10.8
Africa	296	−19.3	−20.9	−11.1
Central and South America	274	−23.7	−15.7	−5.8
South and South-East Asia	690	−9.1	−4.2	−15.5
West Asia	133	−9.8	−14.3	−11.2

[a] mmt − million metric tonnes

EFFECTS ON WORLD FOOD TRADE

Effects on food production

The future without climate change

Assuming no effects of climate change on crop yields, but population growth and economic growth as given on p. 80, world cereal production is estimated at 3286 million metric tons (mmt) in 2060 (cf. 1795 mmt in 1990). The estimate for cereals includes wheat, rice, maize, millet, sorghum and minor grains contained in the FAO AGROSTAT database. Rice is included as rice milled equivalent (a factor of 0.67 is used to convert from rice paddy to milled rice). Cereal prices are estimated at an index of 121 (1970 = 100). The number of people at risk from hunger is estimated at about 640 million (cf. 530 million in 1990).

Effects of climate change, with internal adjustment in the model, but without adaptation

Under the estimated effects of climate change and atmospheric CO_2 on crop yields, the effects on cereal production are given in Table 4.2 and Fig. 4.3. These estimations are based upon dynamic simulations by the BLS that allow the world food system to respond to

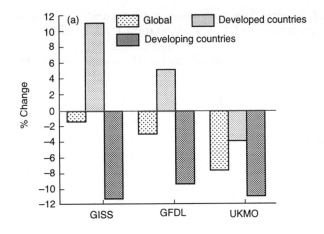

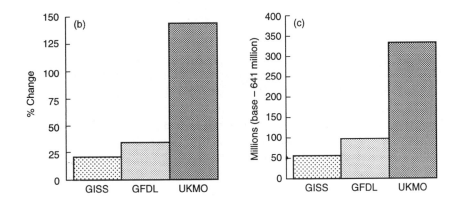

Fig. 4.3 Effects of climate change on cereal production, prices, and number of people at risk from hunger under climate change scenarios in 2060. (a) Change in cereal production; (b) increases in cereal prices; (c) additional number of people at risk from hunger.

climate-induced supply shortfalls of cereals and consequently higher commodity prices through dynamic increases in production factors, cultivated land, labour, and capital, and inputs such as fertilizer. World cereal production is estimated to decrease between 1 and 7 per cent, depending on the GCM climate scenario. Under the UKMO scenario, global production is estimated to decrease by more than 7 per cent, while under the GISS scenario (which assumes lower

Table 4.3 Effects of climate change on production, under two levels of adaptation: adaptation level 1 (AD1) and adaptation level 2 (AD2)

	Changes in cereal production (% of 2060 reference)		
	GISS	GFDL	UKMO
World			
Without adaptation	−1.2	−2.8	−7.6
AD1	0.0	−1.6	−5.2
AD2	1.1	−0.1	−2.4
Developed			
Without adaptation	11.3	5.2	−3.5
AD1	14.2	7.9	3.9
AD2	11.0	3.0	0.8
Developing			
Without adaptation	−11.0	−9.2	−10.8
AD1	−11.2	−9.2	−12.4
AD2	−6.6	−5.6	−5.7

temperature increases) cereal production is estimated to decrease by just over 1 per cent. The largest negative changes occur in developing countries, which average −9 per cent to −11 per cent. By contrast, in developed countries production is estimated to increase under all but the UKMO scenario (+11 per cent to −3 per cent). Thus existing disparities in crop production between developed and developing countries are estimated to increase.

Effects of climate change under different levels of adaptation

Under adaptation level 1

Table 4.3 and Fig. 4.4 show the effects of level 1 adaptation on estimated changes in cereal production. These largely offset the negative climate change yield effects in developed countries, improving their comparative advantage in world markets. In these regions cereal production increases by 4–14 per cent over the reference case. However, developing countries are estimated to benefit little from adaptation (−9 to −12 per cent). Averaged global production is altered 0 to −5 per cent from the reference case. As a consequence, world cereal prices are estimated to increase by *c.* 10–100 per cent, and the number of people at risk from hunger by *c.* 5–50 per cent (see Fig. 4.5). This indicates that level 1 adaptations would have relatively little influence on reducing the global effects of climate change.

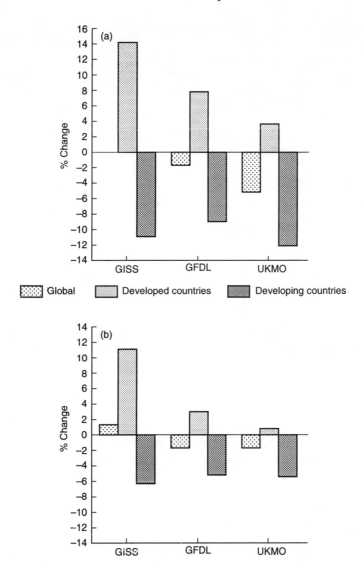

Fig. 4.4 Change in cereal production under climate change scenarios in 2060, assuming different levels of adaptation. (a) Adaptation level 1; (b) adaptation level 2.

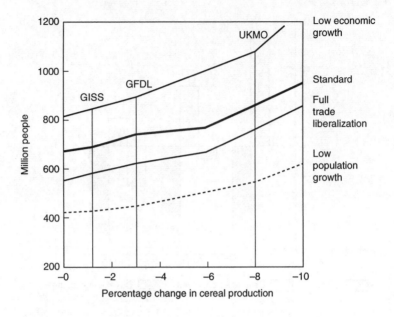

Fig. 4.5 Effects of different assumptions and policies on number of people at risk from hunger.

Under adaptation level 2

More extensive adaptation virtually eliminates negative cereal yield impacts at the global level under the GISS and GFDL climate scenarios and reduces impacts under the UKMO scenario by one-third (see Table 4.3 and Fig. 4.4). However, the decrease in comparative advantage of developing countries under these scenarios leads to decreased cereal acreages in these countries. Cereal production in developing countries still decreases by about 5 per cent. Globally, however, cereal prices increase only by *c.* 5–35 per cent, and the number of people at risk from hunger is altered by between −2 per cent and +20 per cent from the reference case. This suggests that level 2-type adaptations are required to mitigate the negative effects of climate change, and still do not eliminate them in developing countries.

Net imports of cereals into developing countries increase under all scenarios. The change in cereal imports is largely determined by the size of assumed yield change, the change in relative productivity in developed and developing regions, the change in world market prices, and changes in incomes of developing countries. Under the

Table 4.4 Effects of climate change on production assuming full trade liberalization (REF-FTL)

	Ref. (2060) (mmt)	REF-FTL (mmt)	Changes in cereal production in 2060 (% REF-FTL)		
			GISS (%)	GFDL (%)	UKMO (%)
Global	3286	3356	−0.9	−2.6	−8.2
Developed	1449	1472	12.5	6.5	−3.7
Developing	1836	1884	−11.3	−9.7	−11.6

Ref. (2060) assumes no climate change.
REF-FTL, reference 2060 with full trade liberalization and no climate change.
mmt = million metric tons.

GISS climate scenario, productivity is depressed largely in favour of developed countries, resulting in pronounced increases of net cereal imports into developing countries. Under the UKMO scenario, large cereal price increases limit the increase of imports to developing countries. Consequently, despite its beneficial impact for developed countries, the adaptation level 1 scenarios show only little improvement in developing countries compared to the corresponding impacts without such adaptation.

Effects of climate change assuming full trade liberalization, and lower economic and population growth rates

Full trade liberalization

Assuming full trade liberalization in agriculture by 2020 provides for more efficient resource use, leading to a 3.2 per cent higher value added in agriculture globally; and a 5.2 per cent higher agriculture GDP in developing countries (excluding China) by 2060 compared to the reference scenario. This policy change results in almost 20 per cent fewer people at risk from hunger. Global cereal production is up 70 mmt, with most of the production increases occurring in developing countries (see Table 4.4). Global impacts due to climate change are slightly reduced under most climatic scenarios, with enhanced gains in production accruing to developed countries, but losses in production greater in developing countries (see Fig. 4.4). Price increases are reduced slightly from what would occur without full trade liberalization, and the number of people at risk from hunger is reduced by about 100 million.

Table 4.5 Effects of climate change on production assuming a low rate of economic growth (REF-E)

	Ref. (2060) (mmt)	REF-E (mmt)	Changes in cereal production in 2060 (% REF-E)		
			GISS (%)	GFDL (%)	UKMO (%)
Global	3286	3212	−1.0	−2.7	−7.9
Developed	1449	1428	12.5	6.0	−3.6
Developing	1836	1786	−11.6	−9.7	−11.3

Ref. (2060) assumes no climate change.
REF-E, reference 2060 with low economic growth and no climate change.
mmt = million metric tons.

Reduced rate of economic growth

Estimates were also made of impacts under a lower economic growth scenario (10 per cent lower than reference). These are indicated in Fig. 4.5 and Table 4.5. Lower economic growth results in a tighter supply situation, higher prices, and more people below the hunger threshold. Prices are 10 per cent higher and the number of people at risk from hunger is 20 per cent greater. The effect of climate change on these trends is generally to reduce production, increase prices, and increase the number of people at risk from hunger by about the same ratio as in the case with a higher economic growth rate. But the absolute amounts of change are greater.

Altered rates of population growth

The largest impact of any of the considered policies would result from an accelerated reduction in population growth in developing countries (Table 4.6). Simulations based on rates of population growth according to UN low estimates result in a world population about 17 per cent lower in year 2060 when compared to UN mid-estimates as used in the reference run. The corresponding reduction in the developing countries (excluding China) would be about 19.5 per cent from 7.3 billion to 5.9 billion. The combination of higher GDP per capita (about 10 per cent) and lower world population produces an estimated 40 per cent less people at risk from hunger in the year 2060 compared to the reference scenario.

Even under the most adverse of the three climate scenarios (UKMO) the estimated number of people at risk from hunger is some 10 per cent lower than that estimated for the reference scenario

Table 4.6 Effects of climate change on production assuming UN low estimate of population growth (REF-P).

	Ref. scenario (mmt)	REF-P (mmt)	Changes in cereal production in 2060 (% REF-P)		
			GISS (%)	GFDL (%)	UKMO (%)
Global	3286	2929	−0.7	−2.6	−7.1
Developed	1449	1349	10.3	4.8	−3.9
Developing	1836	1582	−10.1	−8.9	−9.9

Reference scenario assumes no climate change.
REF-P, reference 2060 with low economic growth and no climate change.
mmt = million metric tons.

without any climate change. Increases in world prices of agricultural products, in particular of cereals, under the climate change scenarios employing the low population projection are around 75 per cent of those using the UN mid-estimate.

CONCLUSIONS

Climate change induced by increasing greenhouse gases is likely to affect crop yields differently from region to region across the globe. Under the climate change scenarios adopted in this study, the effects on crop yields in mid- and high-latitude regions appear to be less adverse than those in low-latitude regions. However, the more favourable effects on yield in temperate regions depend to a large extent on full realization of the potentially beneficial direct effects of CO_2 on crop growth. Decreases in potential crop yields are likely to be caused by shortening of the crop growing period, decrease in water availability due to higher rates of evapotranspiration, and poor vernalization of temperate cereal crops. When adaptations at the farm level were tested (e.g. change in planting date, switch of crop variety, changes in fertilizer application and irrigation), compensation for the detrimental effects of climate change was more successful in developed countries.

When the economic implications of these changes in crop yields are explored in a world food trade model, the relative ability of the world food system to absorb impacts decreases with the magnitude of the impact. Regional differences in effects remain noticeable:

developed countries are expected to be less affected by climate change than developing economies. Dynamic economic adjustments can compensate for lower-impact scenarios such as the GISS and GFDL climate scenarios but not higher-impact ones such as the UKMO scenario. Prices of agricultural products are related to the magnitude of the climate change impact, and incidence of food poverty increases even in the least negative climate change scenario tested.

When the effects of lower future population and economic growth rates and trade liberalization were tested in the food trade model, reduced population growth rates would have the largest effect on minimizing the impact of climate change. Lower economic growth results in tighter food supplies, and consequently would result in higher rates of food poverty. Full trade liberalization in agriculture, on the other hand, provides for more efficient resource use and would reduce the number of people at risk from hunger by about 100 million (from the reference case of *c.* 640 million in 2060). However, all of the scenarios of future climate adopted in this study increase the estimates of the number of people at risk from hunger.

REFERENCES

Acock, B. and Allen, L. H., Jr (1985). Crop responses to elevated carbon dioxide concentrations. In *Direct effects of increasing carbon dioxide on vegetation* (ed. B. R. Strain and J. D. Cure), pp. 33–97. US Department of Energy, DOE/ER-0238, Washington DC.

Allen, L. H., Jr, et al. (1987). Response of vegetation to rising carbon dioxide: photosynthesis, biomass and seed yield of soybean. *Global Biogeochemical Cycles*, **1**, 1–14.

Cure, J. D. (1985). Carbon dioxide doubling, responses: a crop survey. In *Direct effects of increasing carbon dioxide on vegetation* (ed. B. R. Strain and J. D. Cure), pp. 33–97. US Department of Energy, DOE/ER-0238, Washington DC.

Cure, J. D. and Acock, B. (1986). Crop responses to carbon dioxide doubling: a literature survey. *Agricultural and Forest Meteorology*, **38**, 127–45.

FAO (1988). *1987 Production yearbook*. Food and Agriculture Organization of the United Nations, Statistics Series No. 82, Rome.

Fischer, G., Frohberg, K., Keyzer, M. A., and Parikh, K. S. (1988). *Linked national models: a tool for international food policy analysis*. Kluwer, Dordrecht.

Godwin, D., Ritchie, J. T., Singh, U., and Hunt, L. (1989). *A user's guide to CERES-Wheat — V2.10*. International Fertilizer Development Center, Muscle Shoals, AL.

Godwin, D., Singh, U., Ritchie, J. T., and Alocilja, E. C. (1992). *A user's guide to CERES-Rice*. International Fertilizer Development Center, Muscle Shoals, AL.

Hansen, J., *et al.* (1988). Global climate changes as forecast by the GISS 3-D model. *Journal of Geophysical Research*, **93**, (D8), 9341–64.

Houghton, J. T., Jenkins, G. J., and Ephraums, J. J. (1990). *Climate change: the IPCC scientific assessment*. Cambridge University Press, Cambridge.

IBRD/World Bank (1990). *World population projections*. Johns Hopkins University Press, Baltimore.

International Benchmark Sites Network for Agrotechnology Transfer (IBSNAT) Project (1989). *Decision support system for agrotechnology transfer version 2.1 (DSSAT V2.1)*. Department of Agronomy and Soil Science, College of Tropical Agriculture and Human Resources, University of Hawaii, Honolulu.

Jones, C. A. and Kiniry, J. R. (1986). *CERES-Maize: a simulation model of maize growth and development*. Texas A&M Press, College Station.

Jones, J. W., Boote, K. J., Hoogenboom, G., Jagtap, S. S., and Wilkerson, G. G. (1989). *SOYGRO V5.42: soybean crop growth simulation model. Users' guide*. Department of Agricultural Engineering and Department of Agronomy, University of Florida, Gainesville, FL.

Kimball, B. A. (1983). Carbon dioxide and agricultural yield. An assemblage and analysis of 430 prior observations. *Agronomy Journal*, **75**, 779–88.

Otter-Nacke, S., Godwin, D. C., and Ritchie, J. T. (1986). *Testing and validating the CERES-Wheat model in diverse environments*. AgGRISTARS YM-15-00407. Johnson Space Center 20244.

Pearman, G. (1988). *Greenhouse: planning for climate change*. CSIRO, Canberra.

Peart, R. M., Jones, J. W., Curry, R. B., Boote, K., and Allen, L. H., Jr (1989). Impact of climate change on crop yield in the southeastern U.S.A. In *The potential effects of global climate change on the United States* (ed. J. B. Smith and D. A. Tirpak). US Environmental Protection Agency, Washington DC.

Ritchie, J. T. and Otter, S. (1985). Description and performance of CERES-Wheat: a user-oriented wheat yield model. In *ARS wheat yield project* (ed. W. O. Willis), pp. 159–75. Department of Agriculture, Agricultural Research Service, ARS-38, Washington DC.

Ritchie, J. T., Singh, U., Godwin, D., and Hunt, (1989). *A user's guide to CERES-Maize — V2.10*. International Fertilizer Development Center, Muscle Shoals, AL.

Rosenberg, N. J. and Crosson, P. R. (1991). *Processes for identifying regional influences of and responses to increasing atmospheric CO_2 and climate change: the MINK Project, an overview*. Resources for the Future, Dept of Energy DOE/RL/01830T-H5, Washington, DC.

Rosenzweig, C. and Parry, M. L. (1994). Potential impact of climate change on world food supply. *Nature*, **367**, 133–8.

Smit, B. (1989). Climatic warming and Canada's comparative position in acricultural production and trade. In *Climate Change Digest*, pp. 1–9. CCD 89-01. Environment Canada.

United Nations (1989). *World population prospects 1988*. United Nations, New York.

5

Women: the neglected factor in sustainable development

Pramilla Senanayake

Dr Senanayake has worked for the International Planned Parenthood Federation since 1975. Having served as Medical Director for ten years, in May 1987 she took up the post of Assistant Secretary General for Technical Services, and has overall responsibility for the programme development, medical, AIDS prevention and evaluation functions of the IPPF.

Born in Sri Lanka, Dr Senanayake obtained her medical degree from the University of Colombo, Sri Lanka. She later obtained her Diploma in Tropical Public Health (DTPH) and a PhD at the University of London. She has extensive experience working in developing countries, particularly in Asia and Africa, primarily as a paediatrician and public health specialist.

Dr Senanayake has been closely associated with the development of family planning programmes around the world, and has worked with WHO and other international agencies in developing guidelines on the various methods of fertility regulation and in designing and implementing service delivery programmes.

Her experience in other aspects of family planning work such as developing reproductive health programmes for adolescents, ensuring quality of care in family planning, particularly with regard to women's concerns and perspectives, and in issues relating to the reduction of unsafe abortion is considerable. She also regularly undertakes media related activities which include television broadcasts and radio and press interviews. She is the author of many publications covering family planning, adolescent reproductive health, contraceptive technology, women's perspectives, unsafe abortion, and related topics.

INTRODUCTION

Sustainable development is now a central concern of international relations as well as of national policy. All through human history, the environment has been treated as a 'free good', and there was much logic in this until the early years of the twentieth century. Resources were exploited by the world's people on a modest enough scale for them to be replenishable. However, in the past six to seven decades the rate of consumption has exceeded the rate of replenishment; the gap is widening and our environmental capital is dwindling rapidly.

The poor are the worst affected. For them, the soils, the land, the forests, and the water are their capital and these are being depleted before their very eyes. And among the poor, the women are the worst affected. The role of women in developing countries is critical to sustainable development, since the women play a large role in managing economic, human, social, and environmental resources. Although women are the managers of natural resources they are also neglected, because the institutions of society and of the economy attach primacy of place to men who are considered, irrationally, to be the breadwinners.

It is the basic argument of this paper that sustainable development can only be ensured when women and gender issues are treated with the highest priority. Improving women's conditions can result in major economic, social, and environmental gains, probably at a very low cost in terms of resource allocation. This chapter deals with four main areas: the gender issue as a development variable; the current involvement of women in important productive areas; health, and family planning, and education; and some feasible ways ahead. Because they are so crucial, the chapter concentrates on health, family planning, and education, the areas where women have particularly suffered neglect.

Gender as a development variable

The relevance of social issues in general, and of the gender variable in particular, to conservation and sustainable development efforts is at last becoming acknowledged. Policy-makers are finding that if the differential impacts of planned interventions — on women and men, young and old, privileged and underprivileged — are not taken into account, development programmes are unlikely to succeed: 'The eroding status of low-income women in developing countries is a baseline indicator of human progress. Ignoring this issue is not only morally untenable; it is in the long-run self-defeating. Until gender bias is confronted, there can be no sustainable development' (Jacobson 1992).

Gender is a cross-cutting issue that must be considered in all plans for resource management, since in many societies access to and control over resources are determined by gender. It is necessary to look not only at women's and men's roles in resource management but also at the dynamics of relationships between men and women working together in the society, and to determine how these respective roles will need to change if sustainable development is to be achieved.

A thorough analysis of different social groups and their differential access to, and use of, natural resources is needed in order to understand the dynamics of sustainable or non-sustainable use. Conservation programmes cannot be effectively implemented if the precise target groups and main decision-makers and actors are not known. Gender analysis has been developed in response to the failure of a decade of 'Women in development' policies to improve women's lives through income-generating projects or increased educational opportunities. These types of solutions were not effective as long as basic inequalities between men and women continued to exist and the sexual division of labour was not taken into account (World Conservation Union (IUCN) 1992).

While sex primarily identifies the biological differences between women and men, gender refers to what is socially determined and accepted as being characteristic of a woman or a man. Gender deals with relationships between women and men and the way these relationships are socially shaped and established. A distinction is needed between men's and women's reproductive roles, which are biological, and their gender roles, which are socially determined and can differ according to traditional religious, social, and cultural mores.

Gender roles are also influenced by economic, political, and demographic factors, including migration patterns, infant mortality, life expectancy, and so on. These determinants are important because they shape the scope of people's activities, their access to and control over resources, and the decisions they make about matters concerning their families. They are also important because, unlike reproductive roles, they can be altered. Thus gender needs to be recognized as a development variable. All societies have a gender-based distribution of roles. Understanding the implications and consequences of gender patterns can help in organizational planning and in the design and implementation of programmes which take gender differences into consideration.

Institutions — organizations, policies, practices, and systems — are heavily weighted against women, especially in developing countries. Gender biases in this institutional infrastructure need to be removed in a methodical way. They may be in the area of property rights, credit arrangements, consultative political processes, in systems of health and education, in the social division of labour, in research and development methodologies leading to technological change and innovation. A pervasive feature in all these is that the gender issue is neglected or treated with indifference. That neglect must be overcome.

Poverty

According to a World Bank (1992*a*) review of women's health, two out of three women around the world presently suffer from the most debilitating disease known to humanity—poverty. After four decades of conventional economic development strategies aimed at improving human prospects, the number of people living in poverty continues to grow. More than 1 billion people world-wide live in absolute poverty, defined by the World Bank (1992*b*) as 'a condition of life so limited by malnutrition, illiteracy, disease, squalid surroundings, high infant mortality, and low life expectancy as to be beneath any reasonable definition of human decency'. At least two billion others have incomes insufficient to meet more than their most basic immediate needs. Women are disproportionately represented among these numbers, making poverty the leading cause of death and illness in females.

The health risks of poverty are far greater for females than for males. The United Nations Human Development Index, which measures the extent to which people have the resources to attain a decent standard of living, shows that women have lagged behind men in every country for which data are available. Not only do women not automatically benefit from economic growth, they may even fall further behind. Indeed, women lag behind men on virtually every indicator of social and economic status. In every country and at every socio-economic level, women control fewer productive assets than do men. Women everywhere work longer hours but earn less income despite the fact that they are responsible for meeting 40 to 100 per cent of a family's basic needs. And, lacking alternatives, women are more often compelled to resort to jobs that are seasonal and labour-intensive and which carry considerable occupational risk. As a result, poverty among females is more intractable than among males, and their health even more vulnerable to adverse changes in social and environmental conditions (Koblinsky *et al.* 1992).

The impact of poverty and low social status on women's health is not just an issue for developing countries. In the United States, for instance, lack of access to income and education has had a proven adverse impact on the reproductive health of poor women.

WOMEN AND DEVELOPMENT:
CONTRIBUTIONS AND CONSTRAINTS

Although women's role in development is neglected by policymakers, in most parts of the Third World women are the key to economic and social survival. Women, as agricultural and craft producers, keep poor households going. They grow the crops, gather the firewood, tend the animals, and fetch the water. They are industrial entrepreneurs, through their long handicraft and cottage industry traditions. They are the great invisible workforce whose labour finds no place in national economic statistics because it is unpaid; women are generally and wrongly regarded as unproductive of anything except children.

Women in subsistence economies in the rural areas of Asia, Africa, and Latin America are the major suppliers of food, fuel, and water for their families. They contribute far more than men to food production, the harvesting of forest products, and the management of local energy and water resources. The International Fund for Agricultural Development (IFAD), in a recent report (1992), shows that the number of poor rural women has increased dramatically in the past two decades: 'Notwithstanding the increasing female responsibility for agricultural production and income generation in rural areas, women have least access to means of production, receive the lowest wages, and are the least educated.' The report goes on to conclude: 'The poverty question has thus become inseparable from the gender question.'

Food

It is estimated that in sub-Saharan Africa women grow 80 per cent of the food for their families. Their labour produces 70–80 per cent of food crops in the Indian subcontinent and 50 per cent of the household food in Latin America and the Caribbean. In all regions, about half of all cash crops are cultivated by women farmers and women agricultural labourers (Jacobson 1992).

There is a clear division of labour between men and women in the agricultural sector. Women are generally responsible for sowing, weeding, crop maintenance, and harvesting, as long as these tasks have not been mechanized. Men, on the other hand, look after field preparation. Subsistence agriculture – the growing of food crops – is almost exclusively a woman's task. But women's participation in cash-cropping is increasing. Care of small animals is also often their responsibility (Davidson and Dankelman 1988).

According to Lester Brown of the Worldwatch Institute, the roles of women are critical to reversing the trend in countries where food production is failing to keep pace with population growth. On a global scale, Brown, noting that grain, animal protein, and fish production have all ceased to grow since 1984, concludes that the only sensible option may now be an all-out effort to slow population growth. The first step is to fill the family planning gap by expanding services: 'But unless the world can go beyond that and attack the conditions that foster rapid population growth — namely the discrimination against women and widespread poverty — reversing the decline may not be possible' (Brown 1993). The food question and gender issues are strongly interlinked.

Forest

Women in subsistence economies also manage forest resources and their conservation. For women, trees and forests provide not only biomass for fuel but also fruit and nuts, medicinal plants, herbs, and many other materials, either for consumption or income generation. It is estimated that in rural Africa, for example, 60–80 per cent of all domestic fuel supplies are gathered from forests by women and girls (Jacobson 1992). But these women are losing access to forest resources through privatization of land, lack of credit and extension services, and male veto power over women's decisions. Conversion of forest into cropland, as a result of the spread of cash crops, has also reduced women's access to biomass resources and forced them to go further and further from their homes in search of fuel.

The importance of forest products to women and the role women play in forest management has been ignored by governments and aid agencies alike. It is also important to note the link between population growth and deforestation. Four-fifths of the massive deforestation between 1973 and 1988 was due to population growth (Harrison 1992). The connections between spreading deforestation and women's welfare are multifaceted.

The World Bank (1992b) forecasts that although people will eventually switch to cooking with modern fuels, many hundreds of millions of women will be using biomass for decades. For this reason much importance is attached to the use of improved biomass stoves, which not only save fuel but also reduce domestic pollution and its deleterious effects on women's health. In countries where these stoves have been successfully introduced it is always the women who test and promote them.

Water

At the end of the International Drinking Water Supply and Sanitation Decade 1980–90 more than 1.2 billion people, 30 per cent of the population of developing countries, still had no access to safe water and some 1.8 billion people lacked adequate sanitation. Two billion people are estimated to live in regions of water stress and scarcity, and this number is expected to grow (Planet 21 1993). In most developing countries, the supply of water, vital for the survival and health of the family and for farming, is exclusively the concern of women and children. In rural areas of developing countries, women and children typically spend 3 or more hours a day collecting water, carrying heavy loads, and damaging their own health in the process. Water is essential for human health; most diseases in developing countries are passed on directly or indirectly through water or as a result of insufficient water to keep clean. Women's lack of decision-making power means that men usually decide where the family house is to be located, often without regard for the distance to water sources. Water shortages and lack of sanitation are not only rural problems; they exist in urban centres as well, exacerbated by the rapid rates of migration into cities.

Although it is difficult to calculate accurately the impact of population growth on water quality and supply, the serious land degradation and drought in the Sahel region of sub-Saharan Africa, where population growth is rapid, indicates the severity of the problem. Population growth intensifies the competitive pressure on access to water for its multiple uses. It lowers the potential amount of water available per capita and introduces the risk of conflict over access to water sources. A large part of this burden falls on women.

In 1980, when the Water Decade was launched, the UN called for the full participation of women in planning, implementation, and application of technology for water supply projects. But women's specialist knowledge of water management—where to collect it and how to cope when supplies are scarce—has been consistently neglected in development programmes.

In many countries efforts are now being made to increase access to available water, particularly to groundwater sources, through the introduction of hand pumps and other fairly simple technologies. Women have a central role to play in these reforms. Only recently, however, have systematic efforts been made to involve women in project identification, development, maintenance, and upkeep. The results have generally been encouraging. In an urban slum in Zambia a women's organization improved drainage around public taps.

Women have been trained as caretakers for hand pumps in Bangladesh, India, Kenya, Lesotho, and Sudan. In Mozambique women engineers and pump mechanics perform alongside, and as effectively as, their male counterparts. In Sri Lanka women's co-operatives have been set up to assemble and maintain a locally manufactured hand pump. Women's co-operatives manage communal standpipes and collect money to pay for metered supplies in Honduras, Kenya, and the Philippines. Women who are trained to manage and maintain community water systems often perform better than men because they are less likely to migrate, are more accustomed to voluntary work, and can be better trusted to administer funds honestly (World Bank 1992*b*).

Access to credit, income, and training

As a consequence of their lack of property rights, women enjoy much less access to education, credit, extension services, and technology than do men. A consequence of the neglect of women's roles in sustainable development is that new technologies and agricultural training schemes have been aimed at men, who apply them largely to the production of cash crops, not to the provision of food for their families. Agricultural extension, too, has suffered from gender bias. In Africa, where most farmers are female, the majority of extension officers are male and trained to deal primarily with male farmers. A 1981 survey found that only 3 per cent of agricultural extension agents in sub-Saharan Africa were female, earning less money than their male counterparts. Women are also frequently neglected by agricultural and forestry extension services. When women have been given equal opportunities, they have shown effective leadership in managing natural resources. For example, the GRAMEEN Bank in Bangladesh has proved that access to credit at reasonable interest rates has made a big difference to the condition of even the poorest women.

Labour

Much of the work that women do is invisible because it does not appear in national economic accounting and is often unpaid. Even when women are remunerated for their work, they earn much less than men. Yet in the 1980s women shouldered a large part of the adjustment burden in developing countries. To make up for lost family income, they increased production for home consumption, worked longer hours, slept less, and often ate less. These substantial costs of structural adjustment have gone largely unrecognized and unrecorded (UNFPA 1993*a*). Gender disparities in total hours worked are greatest among the poor; in developing countries women work an average of 12 to 18 hours per day in producing food, managing and harvesting resources, and working at a variety of paid and unpaid activities, compared to 8 to 12 hours for men (Jacobson 1992).

The traditional domestic division of labour ensures that women tend to be the main providers for family needs, even in male-headed households. In subsistence economies, for example, women usually cover between 40 and 100 per cent of a family's basic needs, and this tendency continues when they enter the cash economy; studies on income allocation by gender have found that virtually 100 per cent of cash income earned by women tends to be allocated for household needs, compared with 75 per cent or less of husbands' incomes. Men often spend a large part of their own incomes on alcohol, tobacco, or other consumer products.

In agriculture, men grow cash crops, retaining the income, while women grow subsistence crops to feed the family and devote any additional income to meeting the family's needs for shelter, clothing, and health. In Africa, for instance, women provide an estimated 50–80 per cent of all agricultural and agroprocessing labour (World Bank 1992*b*). The social belief that female children are an economic liability can be countered by the evidence that in many parts of the developing world girls work more than 6 hours a day throughout the year in the fields and at home.

Official statistics on women's participation in the labour force do not give an accurate picture of their real role in developing countries. But they do suggest the extent to which women's potential contribution is used — or wasted — in the formal economy. Female participation in the official labour force is lowest in the Muslim world. In north Africa only 19 per cent of women are in paid work, and 37 per cent in west Asia. In south Asia their participation rate is only 39 per cent. The value of women's full participation in the workforce is clear from east Asia's record of economic growth and human resource development. Here no less than 78 per cent of women are active in the labour force — even higher than the 67 per cent average for developed countries (UNFPA 1992).

Women's access to the labour market brings multiple benefits. It works to lower fertility by delaying the age of marriage. After marriage it provides women with an independent income which improves their power and status in the family. It helps children directly, because far more of women's income than men's goes into the welfare of children. Recent research shows that the proportion of children in poverty is much lower in families where the mother does cash work.

Women's economic opportunities affect desired family size. One analysis of the World Fertility Survey data from 20 developing countries found that female participation in the labour force was the single most important determinant of marital fertility. But women without control over their own fertility have limited opportunities to enter paid employment.

Effects of environmental decline

Women are the first victims of environmental degradation. As population grows and communal lands are privatized for cash crops, women are forced on to marginal lands in search of food and fuel for their families. As forests disappear and wells dry up, they spend longer and longer hours fetching water and searching for fuel and edible forest products.

Since they are the first to be badly affected, it follows that in most parts of the world women are first to notice environmental degradation. Women clean the dirt of air pollution and nurse the children who suffer from it. Yet they usually lack the power to act on their problems. Men control farmland and common land. Men decide whether trees are to be planted or not. Harrison (1992) suggests that where women are in a position to act — or where men share the burdens that make women feel the problems earlier — environmental degradation can be dealt with much sooner. It has been suggested that if African men had to gather fuelwood, or if African women were free to plant trees, deforestation and fuelwood shortage in Africa would be remedied much sooner.

Property rights

Women have title to only 1 per cent of the world's land, yet they produce more than half the world's food (Davidson and Dankelman 1988). Most developing countries have a long history of colonial rule which imposed laws and social structures that were particularly harmful to women. Among these are inheritance laws, legislation on land ownership and transfer, and social restrictions on women which seriously limit their activities and aspirations. These patterns have occurred extensively in Africa, but European laws and customs have also altered the place of women in Central America so as to reduce their power. Inheritance laws and communal rights to land which once allowed access by women have, in many cases, been replaced by title-deed systems which, by law or custom, restrict land ownership to individual men. As population growth and commercialization make land scarce and increasingly valuable, commonly held land is increasingly privatized. In most regions, privatization of land was a deliberate policy, encouraged by the investments of governments, donor agencies, and multinational corporations. Women are prevented by legal and cultural obstacles from obtaining title to land and participating in cash-crop cultivation; having no access to credit, they have no means to enhance agricultural productivity. They are further discriminated against when men obtain the best land for themselves, leaving women to feed their families from already exhausted fields. Technologies, irrigation outlets for instance, are introduced to favour lands devoted to cash crops.

Land is less likely to be over-used if its owners have a clear legal title. People who have secure rights to the land they cultivate are more likely to take the long view in managing the soil. They are more likely to have access to formal credit and to invest more in their land. One of the few detailed studies of the connection between greater security and improved land management, conducted in Thailand, shows a clear positive link between more secure tenure, access to formal credit, and investment in the land (World Bank 1992*b*). But security is not synonymous with individual possession of a formal title. In sub-Saharan Africa, in particular, greater security could be achieved by strengthening indigenous and customary land rights. The benefits extend well beyond soil conservation by individual farmers. Legal definition and enforcement of group rights have proved important for improving the management of such common property as grazing land (World Bank 1992*b*).

Some indigenous systems of communal tenure may be flexible enough to evolve with increasing scarcity of land and the commensurate need for greater security of land rights. Lasting solutions to problems of land tenure must, however, remove discrimination against women.

Resource management

International agencies and governments have ignored the part that women play in caring for the environment and the knowledge and experience they can contribute to this process. Women have traditionally practised ecologically sustainable cultivation of communal lands. They are custodians of indigenous knowledge and possess much valuable knowledge about soil conservation, the need to preserve genetic diversity, and the role of trees in watershed management. Because of their responsibilities for securing food, fuel, and water, and the labour this requires, women often have a greater interest in conserving croplands, forests, and other natural resources. Development programmes that vest control over natural resources solely in men are, in effect, supporting short-term consumption at the expense of long-term sustainability (Jacobson 1992). (Conversely, however, it should also be recognized that the burden of women's work leaves little time for additional conservation activities.)

Using traditional methods, women farmers have been quite effective in conserving soil resources. Given access to appropriate resources, they employ fallowing, crop rotation, intercropping, mulching, and other soil conservation techniques. They have played a leading role in maintaining crop diversity. In sub-Saharan Africa, for instance, women are reported to cultivate as many as 120 different plants in the spaces alongside men's cash crops. In some countries of Latin America, women develop and maintain the seed banks on which food production depends (Jacobson 1992).

Women have a strong interest in tree planting and soil conservation because the proximity of sources of firewood determines much of their work burden. In addition, the effect of trees and of soil cover or terracing on infiltration of rain into the soil affects water springs. Deforestation and soil erosion result in more runoff and the drying up of streams, thus increasing women's work burdens.

It should be possible to build on this interest and teach women about these linkages to help and encourage them to plant trees and conserve soil. If such teaching were linked to efforts in improving health, nutrition, and family planning, it would effect improvement across the board in women's lives. The linkage has the advantage that receptivity to change in one area often translates to other areas of life too.

The link between family planning and women's capacity for management of natural resources should be clear. Repeated pregnancies, close together, weaken the health of women, reducing their ability to fulfil their roles as resource managers. Faced with a constant struggle for daily survival, people will use natural resources differently, and with less consideration for longer-term conservation, than those people who depend on natural resources for survival but whose basic needs have been taken care of.

It is therefore important to evaluate the relationship between, on the one hand, the basic problems and daily pressures of poverty and how these result in non-sustainable use of natural resources, and on the other hand, how the lack of access to the basic needs of human life are related to the aggravation of poverty and social and economic problems. It is also important to evaluate the direct impact of natural resources management on the health of the populations concerned and vice versa, including the effect on the morbidity and mortality of infants and young children and the relationship with levels of fertility.

Family size and resource use

Changes in family size lead to changes in per capita resource demand. Large families have a high resource demand as a unit but low per capita use. As family size declines, aspirations rise, leading to more affluent resource use. Ultimately, the total resource use of small families will exceed that of large families, at least in the short run or until ways have been found to reduce overall consumption.

This is a complex issue for sustainable development. In many countries, the decline in mortality is followed eventually by a decline in fertility, but the demographic momentum in the time lag between these two events means that the number of families will have increased. Thus increase in resource consumption per capita multiplied by increased numbers of families will result in a greatly increased resource demand to satisfy basic needs, with a consequent risk of even greater environmental degradation. Obviously, the sooner the demographic transition to smaller families occurs, the smaller will be the total number of families.

Social and cultural obstacles

As is obvious from the discussion above, social and economic discrimination against women are the most formidable obstacles to women's participation in sustainable development. They have negative consequences for the conduct of women's lives in all spheres. They perpetuate high, uncontrolled fertility which in turn limits women's options for any activity outside the home.

Many taboos against women are enshrined in laws that legitimize the inequality of the sexes. Laws also restrict women's access to relevant medical services where, for example, married women are required to obtain their husbands' permission before receiving contraceptive services or undergoing voluntary sterilization. Abortion laws are a case in point. Between 25 and 31 million legal abortions were performed world-wide in 1987. There were at least 10 million illegal attempts to end unwanted pregnancies, and some rough estimates are much higher. Women resort to abortion everywhere, despite restrictive laws or religious opposition. Only 23 per cent of the world's population live in countries where the law permits abortion for social and social-medical reasons, while 25 per cent of the world's population live in countries where abortions are available only when a woman's life is in danger.

Discrimination shows up in laws regulating the age of marriage. Younger ages are fixed for women than for men, leading women into early childbearing and denying them the extra years of education and preparation for life. Girls are often married as young as 13 and commonly by the age of 16 in many developing countries, thus ensuring a very long reproductive life with its consequent health risks. The absence of laws protecting women's health leaves the way open for adolescent pregnancy and high rates of maternal mortality and morbidity.

Women derive their status primarily from their childbearing role and their value is often measured by the number of sons they bear. Preference for sons is strong in many countries. Girls are often considered an economic liability. In India, for example, the dowry tradition imposes a financial burden on the parents of girls. When this is added to lack of property rights and control over economic resources, it is difficult for a woman to provide financial support for ageing parents and therefore she is undervalued by them. The practice of purdah denies women access to the outside world and prevents them from forming partnerships with other women to improve their condition.

Because of the perception that girls are a drain on family resources, families are often unwilling to invest in daughters. Several studies have shown that male children are breastfed longer and receive more and better food and more timely health care than females.

In the sphere of reproductive health, religion and politics have taken precedence over public health concerns. In recent decades, for example, women in the former Soviet Union and much of eastern Europe relied heavily on unsafe abortion because of the enforced scarcity of suitable contraceptives and safe abortion services, a policy intended to increase birth rates. Similarly, in the United States and elsewhere, women's legal right to safe abortion services is now threatened (World Bank 1992*a*).

The opposition of the Roman Catholic Church to the use of modern contraceptives is a major stumbling block. Many priests in Roman Catholic countries recognize the health and economic problems their parishioners face and do not stand in the way of family planning programmes; and many millions of practising Catholics defy the church on contraception. But the position of the Vatican has inhibited some governments from embarking on full-scale, nation-wide family planning programmes and has had an often disastrous effect on the international community, as when the Reagan Administration wiped out all funding for the United Nations Population Fund (UNFPA) and the International Planned Parenthood Federation (IPPF) in 1985 (now restored by the Clinton Administration). The Vatican's continuing opposition to family planning has been restated in a new encylical *Veritatis Splendor.*

Indigenous peoples

Special concern has recently been expressed for indigenous communities in many parts of the world, whose lifestyles and traditions are being eroded by development and who are at risk of being expelled from their traditional homelands.

Indigenous women are the ones that plant, cultivate, and gather the majority of their communities' food, and the ones that keep traditional medicine alive. They are the protectors and central agents for the transmission of culture and language, and keepers of extensive knowledge. Strategies for sustainability call particularly for the empowerment of indigenous women, who have been more adversely affected than men by the process of modernization and the change-over to market economies.

Indigenous women are frequently at the forefront of struggles against destructive development schemes. They see, with considerable justification, that their very survival depends on maintaining the integrity of the land, forests, and other resources, and the maintenance of their traditional access to these resources.

A workshop held in 1993 under the auspices of the World Conservation Union (IUCN) found that recognition of indigenous women's customary and communal rights has often been ignored in land use planning and changes in allocation of property rights. Use and access rights are very important and the ignoring of these rights has served to increase the negative effects of many forms of development assistance. Participatory and group-based methods have proved effective in improving the productivity of indigenous women, by giving them access to credit, inputs, markets, and an expanded voice in decisions that are made. The workshop concluded that, in order to identify interventions to strengthen their productive capacity, mechanisms must be in place to gather gender-specific information at the family and community level.

Migrants

It is mistakenly assumed that most people who migrate internally and internationally are men, and immigration policies generally assume that migrants are men. However, according to UNFPA (1993*b*) estimates, 75 per cent of the total global refugee population may be women and 60–80 per cent of refugee households are headed by women.

Case studies in different regions of the developing world show that many women are forced to flee from inhospitable environments from which a livelihood can no longer be produced. In their new circumstances they find the lowest-paid jobs and their employment status declines more rapidly than that of men.

When men migrate, leaving women behind with no title to land, women may have no choice but to migrate as well in search of employment. According to the United Nations, there is a direct link in developing countries between internal and international migration and the increase in female headed households. Young women are often encouraged to migrate as part of their families' strategy for survival. In Asia and Latin America, female migrants tend to come from large families.

Refugees are notoriously ill-served by health and social services, particularly reproductive health services. Thus female refugees are put at increased risk of unwanted pregnancies that threaten their fragile hold on employment possibilities. And since economic incentives are lacking for women, this is yet another area where the potential contribution of women to sustainable development is being ignored.

Misguided development policies

Gender-blind governments and aid agencies have failed to acknowledge the contribution of women to economic productivity and to take measures to capitalize on their potential. The low status of women in almost every society, lack of access to credit and to the ownership of property is perpetuated by their virtual absence from participation in the decision-making process. National and international development policies have received only scant input in recent years from women's very special creativities and energies. Women are seldom consulted in the design and implementation of development programmes. Their needs are not addressed, nor is their accumulated knowledge recognized and used. As already noted, official statistics usually ignore the value of women's work, reinforcing the impression that women fail to contribute as much as men. As a result, policymakers in most countries invest far less in their female workers than in the males. Donor agencies follow suit (Jacobson 1992).

The real economic and social benefits derived from women's work contrast sharply with the perception that women are unproductive. Development programmes have been built on the premise that what is good for men is good for the family. Conventional development strategies tend to assume that household members share a common standard of living. In reality, women and men may operate in separate economies, and indicators of well-being may differ widely between female and male family members (UNFPA 1993*b*).

HEALTH AND FAMILY PLANNING, AND EDUCATION

I have argued that a multifaceted approach to economic and social change is essential and urgently needed in order to improve the condition of women and, thereby, to facilitate sustainable development. I now focus on two critical areas: health and family planning, and education. There are several reasons why these two areas should be considered for priority attention. These are the obvious priorities in any public policies that attach importance to the humane treatment of women. Health, control over their reproductive capacities, and education are the preconditions for women to be socially and economically active. Women in developing countries are largely inarticulate and backward because they lack these essentials. In fact, health and education are among the most neglected human rights of women. Health and family planning, and education are the areas through which women can be empowered to seek their own fortunes and destiny, and reduce the burdensome dependence that they suffer from. Third, it is attention to these areas that can make women efficient managers of environmental resources and of the household economy, including bringing up the next generation as useful citizens. It is proven that the highest rates of social return from investments are in the area of women's education, and making them literate. Finally, providing women with opportunities for health and family planning, and education should generate major increases in economic productivity, in view of their important economic role. It is the best mechanism for growth and redistribution, blended into one.

Health: the critical factor

Sustainable development depends on healthy participants. The widespread neglect of women's health contrasts sharply with the growing perception of women as agents of change. The participation of women in sustainable development, therefore, demands dramatic improvements in their general and reproductive health.

In many developing countries, the discrimination against women is reflected in their poor health status compared to men. From the beginning of their lives, different feeding practices, additional burdens of work, and lack of basic education put girls at greater risk than boys of malnutrition and disease. Other practices, such as early marriage, force women into the reproductive cycle before they are physically and socially mature, leading to repeated pregnancies, often at the risk of their lives (World Health Organization (WHO) 1992*a*).

The parameters of women's health are ill-defined. The real magnitude of women's medical problems is still unknown, as also are the means to address many of the problems. But there are areas where the problems are known and so are the interventions. Poverty and powerlessness constitute serious health hazards, and these are two problems from which women suffer disproportionately. The problems for baby girls begin soon after birth and continue through childhood, when malnourishment and poor education make girls more likely than boys to suffer from ill-health and lack of opportunity. This discrimination continues through adolescence, early marriage and premature childbearing.

Value orientations in communities, in some instances backed up by legislation, have contributed to preferential treatment of males. With very little being invested to change these values, women have had little choice but to accept the perpetuation of these value systems and the accompanying discriminatory practices. These include, in addition to the differential feeding practices mentioned above, the preference given to boys in seeking medical help and services. Feelings of powerlessness, fear, societal taboos, and other factors rooted in value systems inhibit women's ability to express their own pain and suffering resulting from illness, violence, and discriminatory practices (WHO 1992*b*).

Huge gaps continue to exist in our understanding of women's health on either side of the reproductive years. Adolescence marks a time in a woman's life when improved health status and adequate growth could help buffer the future demands of such energy-intensive activities as heavy manual labour or childbearing. Awareness of the problems of menopausal and ageing women is also needed. Similarly, non-maternal, non-reproductive health needs during the reproductive years have received scant attention (World Bank 1992*a*).

Rapid rates of population growth in many countries, as well as other perceived national priorities, have defeated the efforts of governments to provide adequate health and social services. Just as there is increasing recognition that health is essential to socio-economic development; just as in a growing number of countries the high-level national leadership accepts health as a part of overall socio-economic development and a powerful contribution to such development; just as there is a much greater political commitment in both industrialized and developing countries to promoting and securing people's health; and just as the world international community is speaking more with one voice; so many developing countries are faced with a serious economic crisis, which keeps health programmes at a low level of investment. Health budgets in developing countries are typically less than 1 per cent of total national expenditure.

Fortunately, not all countries have taken a narrow path to development. There are countries in both the industrialized and the developing world whose development agendas place high priority on equity and social justice in health; whose accomplishments, as a consequence of the marriage of scientific knowledge, appropriate technology, and political commitment backed up with sound infrastructure, represent an inspiration and an example of what can be accomplished with relatively limited resources in a short time, given innovation, motivation and appropriate management. Countries such as Sweden, Canada, Sri Lanka, and Zimbabwe illustrate what can be achieved.

General indicators

As partners for safe motherhood have stated, 'A woman's health is her total well-being, not determined solely by biological factors and reproduction, but also by effects of workload, nutrition, stress, war and migration, among others' (World Bank 1992*a*).

Global average life expectancy among females rose from 49 years in the period 1950–55 to 66 years in 1985–90. But indications are that even where women are living longer they may be suffering more. The vast majority of women world-wide continue to suffer the effects of chronic overwork, inadequate nutrition, frequent childbearing, and emotional stress.

Aggregate statistics mask important qualitative differences in life expectancy between males and females. Mortality rates for young girls are higher than those for males in a number of countries throughout the Middle East, North Africa, and the Indian subcontinent. This results from, among other things, gender discrimination in the allocation of food and health care coupled with high rates of death from complications of pregnancy and childbirth, all of which reflect the low socio-economic status of women in these regions.

Edstrom (1992) argues that the maternal mortality rate does not capture the full medical risk which women face in their role as reproducers of the human race. He proposes the concept of lifetime risk, which takes into account both the risk of individual childbirths and the average number of children women produce in a lifetime. Maternal mortality is also often the end result of a life diminished by discrimination from the moment of birth to early marriage. Indeed, death may come as a release for women who live in miserable poverty and whose full personhood is denied by custom, status and lack of access to education, medical care and self-determination.

Parental preference for male children often manifests itself in neglect, deprivation, or discriminatory treatment of girls to the detriment of their mental and physical health. It may mean that a female child is disadvantaged from birth. Nutrition, care during sickness, education, and labour practices are but a few of the areas where sons benefit more than daughters, resulting in higher female childhood mortality. It is estimated that neglect and discrimination against female children leads to serious consequences which account for between 500 000 and 1 million deaths among female children each year.

Reproductive health

The reproductive health of poor women in the developing countries is appalling. Maternal mortality and morbidity rates are from 10 to 100 times higher than for women in developed countries, the biggest differential in any socio-economic measurement contrasting developed and developing societies. An estimated 500 000 women die each year from pregnancy-related causes and another 100 million suffer morbidities or long-term disabling diseases. At these rates, unwanted and high-risk pregnancies are killing more than 1300 women world-wide every day. Obviously, therefore, a woman's ability to control her fertility is a major element in allowing her to improve her own and her family's prospects for the future, including her chances of participating in sustainable resource management. If women are not freed from the excessive health risks they bear, the greatest resource for sustainable development will be wasted (UNFPA 1993*a*).

The maternal mortality rate is today the predominant indicator for reporting on women's health in developing countries. WHO defines maternal death as the death of a woman whilst pregnant or within 42 days of delivery or termination of pregnancy, from any cause related to or aggravated by the pregnancy or its management. Most direct obstetric deaths are caused by haemorrhage, infections, tox-aemia, obstructed labour, or complications from spontaneous or induced abortion. These account for about three-quarters of mater-nal deaths in the Third World; if anaemia, which is an indirect cause, is included, the proportion rises to about 80 per cent.

Fifteen million children in developing countries die every year before the age of 5 years. One of the major causes of child death is the mother's poor reproductive health, which reduces the child's chances of survival. If a mother is malnourished her low-birth-weight child has a far greater chance of being weak and of contrac-ting illnesses resulting in death. Of the nearly 130 million infants born each year, 20 million (16 per cent) have a low birth weight; 95 per cent of such infants are born in developing countries.

Where total fertility rates are high, women tend to experience their first pregnancy early in life, which increases the risks associated with first births. High total fertility rates also often coincide with con-tinued childbearing into older ages and larger total numbers of births per woman mean shorter intervals between pregnancies. Each of these aspects implies increased risk to maternal health.

The reproductive system is particularly sensitive to adverse environmental conditions. Every stage of the multi-step process of reproduction can be disrupted by external environmental agents and this may lead to increased risk of abortion, birth defects, fetal growth retardation, and perinatal death. An increase in the level of harmful chemicals in breast milk has recently been documented. Environmental factors have been cited as a cause of the decrease over the last 50 years of the concentration of sperm in the semen of apparently normal men (Fathalla 1992).

Some environmental pollutants, both natural and man-made (e.g. chlorinated hydrocarbons) mimic the effects of oestrogen (female sex hormone), and there is growing concern that prenatal and postnatal exposure to these chemicals may cause potentially harmful changes in the reproductive system. Stress from different environmental sources can contribute, among other things, to infertility, sexual dysfunction, and lower immune defences.

Sexually transmitted diseases (STDs) continue to occur at

unacceptably high levels all over the world. Urbanization, unemployment, economic hardship, and a relaxation of traditional restraints on sexual activity have been blamed for the intransigence of this situation, as well as the emergence of antibiotic-resistant strains of micro-organisms. In the last decade of the twentieth century the world is facing a serious challenge to human survival which, in some ways, supersedes the challenge of human development. This crisis is no more evident than in the struggle against AIDS (acquired immunodeficiency syndrome)—a struggle which is particularly relevant for women in the developing world. For these women AIDS is a scourge that exploits their poverty, their lack of proper health care, their higher risk of infection, and ultimately their lack of power to control their lives.

In addition, other sexually transmitted diseases also affect women, and the risk of transmission is greater from man to woman than vice versa. Serious sequelae of STDs affect women more than they do men. These include pelvic inflammatory disease, infertility, ectopic pregnancy, and cancer of the cervix. In addition, women can transmit the disease to the fetus.

Adolescent health

For female adolescents, having children at an early age presents serious health and social problems. Their future educational, employment, and social opportunities may be severely curtailed. Teenage pregnancy is a serious health problem in many countries. In both developed and developing countries, early childbearing increases the chances of medical complications. Adolescent mothers are twice as likely to die during childbirth than women in their early twenties. In many developing countries complications of pregnancy, childbirth, and the puerperium are among the main causes of death in between the ages of 15 and 19. The death rate from causes related to abortion and delivery is particularly high in girls below 18 years of age. In both developed and developing countries too many women become mothers too soon for their own welfare and that of their children. Early marriage and childbearing are closely linked to high total fertility. Women who marry between the ages of 15 and 19 are likely to bear, on average, six or seven children.

Births to women under 20 represent an increasing proportion of all births, a fact partially explained by the comparatively greater number of young people in the populations of developing countries. The number of young people under the age of 15 in the population of the world as a whole grew from 700 million in 1950 to 1.7 billion in 1990. The highest rates of increase occur in the developing countries, with 40 per cent of the population under the age of 15 in east, central and west Africa, and 39 per cent in southern Asia (UNFPA 1993*a*). Such figures indicate the trend in numbers of young women entering reproductive age.

Patterns of sexual behaviour in many societies are being altered by biological, social, and economic factors. Among these, early sexual maturity, changing moral values, and later marriage figure prominently. Migration from village to town or from one country to another, and the influence of the mass media, have in some countries lessened the influence of social mechanisms which formerly discouraged adolescent sexual activity before marriage. An increase in cases of sexually transmitted diseases is being reported among young people.

Both traditional and modern societies expose very young women to unwanted pregnancy, which can ruin their entire lives by cutting off forever their chances of education, employment, and personal self-fulfilment. It is essential that young people of both sexes should be carefully prepared for responsible parenthood through appropriate sex and family life education in and out of school. Services for young women are needed which cater to their special needs and protect them from exploitation.

Family planning

Fertility regulation is central to all other aspects of reproductive health. It contributes to the prevention of sexually transmitted diseases, and has consequences for unwanted pregnancy, infertility, sexuality, child survival, and safe motherhood. Family planning saves the lives of women and children and, by reducing family size, hastens the demographic transition to population stabilization. Above all, it gives women control over the one part of their own bodies which otherwise eludes them.

In industrialized countries with stable or declining populations, modern contraception is widely practised and a range of contraceptive options is readily available. A revolution in contraceptive technology in the past few decades has produced safe and effective methods, of which the Pill and the intrauterine device are the most widely used. Injectables and sub-dermal implants are gaining in popularity. Condoms, while less effective than hormonal contraceptives, are the main method for men and popular as a prophylactic. Both male and female sterilization is common for those who have completed their desired family size.

Many millions of couples and individuals still do not have access to family planning either because they lack information or because appropriate methods, counselling, and follow-up services are not available. Data from the World Fertility Survey 1984 revealed that 300 million couples who wanted no more children were not practising modern contraception. The real figure is probably as high as 500 million, when unmarried women, those seeking abortions, and dissatisfied users are taken into account.

In many developing countries, family planning services are still not widely available, mainly because of lethargic government attitudes to the provision of health care in general and ignorance about the social and economic benefits to be derived from its promotion. Lack of services correlates with high rates of population growth, high maternal and child mortality, poverty, and the rapid degradation of natural resources.

Nevertheless, there are signs of improvement. Use of modern contraception rose from less than 10 per cent in the 1960s to 45 per cent in 1983 and to 51 per cent in 1992. (UNFPA 1993*a*). The total fertility rate—the average number of children per woman—in developing countries declined from 6.1 in 1965–70 to 3.9 in 1985–90 with, however, great regional differences.

The statistics on induced abortions provide another indication of the level of unmet need for family planning in developing countries. It is estimated that between 36 and 53 million induced abortions are performed each year, an annual rate of between 32 and 46 abortions per 1000 women of reproductive age. In countries with repressive legislation many of these abortions are clandestine, and the exact number is impossible to determine. But it is estimated that out of the 500 000 maternal deaths that occur each year throughout the world as many as one-quarter to one-third may be the result of complications from unsafe abortion procedures (Fathalla 1992).

In all parts of the world, a small but increasing proportion of abortion seekers are unmarried adolescents; in some urban centres in Africa they represent the majority. WHO estimates that more than half of the deaths caused by induced abortion occur in South and South-East Asia, followed by sub-Saharan Africa.

There is indisputable evidence that the risks associated with childbearing are considerably reduced when births are spaced, and when women have children neither too early nor too late. Thus family planning saves children's lives by making possible a proper interval between the birth of siblings. One out of five infant deaths in developing countries—there are more than 8 million deaths of infants under 1 year of age annually—would be prevented if all births were spaced by an interval of at least 2 years.

In summary, the contribution of family planning to saving the lives of infants and children is highly significant. The contraceptive use has direct and indirect benefits because it allows very young women whose infants are prone to higher mortality to delay childbearing until a later age; it allows older and especially high parity women, whose infants are at considerably higher risk of dying, to stop having babies; it contributes to longer intervals between births, which have been found to improve infant and child survival; it reduces maternal mortality; it changes the environment in which couples set their family size goals; and finally it provides a cost-effective route to reducing infant and child mortality.

Family planning programmes have understandably focused on women, since their health risks are so high and their independence so compromised by repeated childbearing. But the reality of women's lives shows that their partners have considerable influence and control in determining whether or not a woman is allowed to use a contraceptive. A woman's access to contraceptive services is often dependent upon the consent of her partner, who may have little knowledge of the benefits to her and her children or may see threats to his own masculinity. In these circumstances, a woman may have little chance of changing entrenched male attitudes.

The history of the family planning movement is quite short. The International Planned Parenthood Federation (IPPF), the leading pioneer world-wide, celebrated its 40th anniversary in 1992. The United Nations General Assembly, after much controversy, finally agreed to meet requests for assistance from developing countries only in 1962. The World Health Organization (WHO) established a Human Reproduction Unit in 1965 and the first population fund was established in 1967, the precursor of what became the United Nations Fund for Population Activities and is now the United Nations Population Fund (UNFPA). More recent advances at the international level have been the commitment of the World Bank and Unicef. Much of the stimulus for the involvement of these agencies has come from the donor community, whose member governments finance family planning activities as part of their development assistance.

EDUCATION: THE ESSENTIAL PRECONDITION

Improved education for girls may be the most important long-term environmental policy in the developing world. Educated women have smaller families and their children tend to be healthier and better educated. Furthermore, since, as we have seen, women are often the principal managers of natural resources, better education will help them to use natural resources more productively and to depend less on natural resources for income. Educated women will have more opportunities for productive off-farm employment – a vital source of income as the average sizes of farms shrink.

Investments in female education have some of the highest returns for development and for the environment. Evidence from a cross-section of countries shows that where no women are enrolled in secondary education, the average woman has seven children, but where 40 per cent of all women have had a secondary education, the average drops to three children, even after controlling for factors such as income.

Education has been emphasized as pivotal in contributing to improving the health behaviour of women and their families. It has been acclaimed as a principal means of improving women's status by opening up options and employment opportunities, by developing leadership capabilities, and by helping women to communicate with other women and groups in society. So far, judging by the educational levels of women of all ages as compared with those of men, actions to reverse the discrimination against women have been unsatisfactory and are a continuing cause for concern (WHO 1992*a*).

While use of family planning is higher with increased education, it is also true that family planning and lower fertility also help to improve women's status and education. When girls leave school early for marriage and childbearing, as they often do in southern Asia and Africa, it perpetuates the cycle of low status and high fertility. Pregnancy outside marriage is a major cause of girls dropping out of school in Latin America and Africa (UNFPA 1992).

Lack of education has been cited as a major contributor to the feminization of poverty. Women bear the final responsibility for children and the family and they continue to accept any job, even one that is low paid and fraught with health risks, in order to ensure their own survival and that of their dependants. Education is understood as encompassing all levels of formal and non-formal education. When educational programmes are designed, the content itself reflects biases and discrimination in society.

It has been estimated that in developing countries each extra year of education for a mother reduces her children's mortality risk by an average of between 7 and 9 per cent. Better education for mothers also reduces the incidence of stunting and underweight in children. Better-educated mothers are more likely to have had tetanus immunization and many times more likely to use antenatal care.

Literacy

The gender gap shows up again in adult literacy. In 1987, while 83 per cent of women were literate in Latin America and 66 per cent in East Asia, in the Arab states the female literacy rate was only 38 per cent. In Africa it was 36 per cent and in southern Asia only 32 per cent. Out of the world's 949 million illiterates in 1985, 592 million — almost two-thirds — were women (UNFPA 1992).

Women are benefiting less than men from improvements in levels of literacy. In 1985, 60 per cent of the adult population world-wide was able to read, compared to about 46 per cent in 1970, but literacy rose faster among men than among women so that the gender gap actually widened. Between 1970 and 1985 the number of women unable to read rose by 54 million, while that of men increased by only 4 million. Of the total adult female population, illiteracy runs at 78 per cent in Bangladesh, 66 per cent in India, 87 per cent in Nepal, and 79 per cent in Pakistan (UNFPA 1992).

Women's inability to read instructions on a packet of contraceptive pills or a diarrhoea remedy, a seed catalogue or an invoice, a will or a newspaper, bars them from the full benefits of development and prevents them from making their full contribution.

There is a strong correlation between illiteracy and large families. In Pakistan, where only 21 per cent of women can read and write, women bear on average 5.9 children. Sri Lanka has a very similar GNP, but 84 per cent of women are literate and women there have on average just 2.5 children (Central Television 1992).

School enrolment

Equal access to education for girls and women is one of the most critical components in efforts to reduce poverty and high fertility. It has been demonstrated that women with seven or more years of education marry, on average, more than 5 years later than women without any education and have between two and three fewer children. Nevertheless, secondary enrolment levels for girls remain low, ranging from 52 per cent in Latin America, to 26 per cent in Asia and 14 per cent in Africa. An estimated 60 per cent of the global total of 105 million children excluded from schools are girls (UNFPA 1991).

Education and smaller families go together. Poorly educated women in Brazil, for instance, have an average of 6.5 children each; those with secondary education only 2.5. In Liberia, women who have been to secondary school are ten times more likely to take advantage of family planning facilities than those who have not been to school at all (UNFPA 1991).

In sub-Saharan Africa only three out of five girls were enrolled in primary school in 1988, and in southern Asia three out of four. In the developing world as a whole only 65 per cent of girls are in primary school, compared with 78 per cent of boys. At secondary school, the gap is even wider, with 37 per cent of girls and 48 per cent of boys attending. Female enrolment at secondary level ranged from only 14 per cent in Africa and 26 per cent in Asia, to 52 per cent in Latin America (Harrison 1992). In Pakistan and the Yemen Arab Republic there are over three times as many boys as girls in secondary school. Malnourished and poorly educated girls are less likely to find well-paid employment than their brothers. Thus they will go on to relive their own mothers' destinies, trapped in a web of low status and high birth rates.

Raising the primary school enrolment rate for girls to equal that for boys in low-income countries would mean educating an additional 25 million girls each year, at a total annual cost of approximately $US950 million. Raising the secondary school enrolment of girls to equal the rate for boys would mean educating an additional 21 million girls at a total cost of $US1.4 billion a year. Eliminating educational discrimination in low-income countries would thus cost a total of $US2.4 billion a year, or about 0.25 per cent of these countries' GDP (World Bank 1992*b*).

Investment in schools, teachers, and materials is essential. But so, too, are policies to encourage enrolment, such as scholarship programmes. In Bangladesh a scholarship programme has succeeded in almost doubling female secondary enrolment, as well as promoting higher labour force participation, later marriage, and lower fertility rates.

It should be clear from the foregoing discussion that if sustainable development is to be achieved, development programmes must be introduced which increase women's control over income and household resources, recognize and improve their productivity, establish their legal and social rights, and increase their access to family planning, health care, education, and economic choices. It is likely that immediate gains could be realized by increasing women's access to land, credit, and the tools and appropriate technologies with which they can increase their own and their families' welfare. Concomitant upon this, however, is their right and ability to decide the number and spacing of their children and to take charge of their own reproductive health.

THE WAY AHEAD

How should we proceed to address gender issues in the context of sustainable development? Many thoughts are contained in the preceding sections. In conclusion I give a brief description of the decisions and strategies of multilateral bodies, especially those of the UN system, which facilitate the selection of the key issues on which the international community needs to focus. Finally I turn the spotlight on a few selected priority areas for action, urgently required for any serious involvement with gender issues.

International strategies

In looking at international strategies a word of qualification is in order. While global strategies are important, it must be recognized that many developing countries have practised what UN resolutions and other global bodies preach for a considerable time. The condition of women and standards of education and health are reasonably satisfactory in Sri Lanka, the Indian state of Kerala, and a few other parts of the developing world. Much has been achieved in recent years in drawing public and political attention to the discrimination against women and the tragic consequences for them and for the world at large of ignoring their existing and potential contributions to sustainable development.

The 1972 International Conference on the Environment virtually ignored the roles of women and rejected population and family planning from its agenda. Surprisingly, the World Commission on Environment and Development — the so-called Brundtland Commission — which made its report in 1987, listed measures, including family planning, to raise the status of women but gave these no special priority.

By contrast, the United Nations Decade for Women 1975–85 unleashed the energies of hundreds of non-governmental organizations (NGOs) which worked on recommendations to governments and international agencies and conferences. The initial response from many governments was to recognize but then marginalize women's issues by the establishment of women's bureaux or, in the donor community, 'women in development' projects which still left women outside the mainstream development process.

In 1985 a United Nations conference on women, held in Nairobi, made a thorough review of progress during the decade and found a great deal still wanting. With advice and pressure from NGOs, the conference adopted 'Forward-looking strategies to the year 2000'

(United Nations 1985). These strategies recognized women's roles as environmental managers and called for their rights to property, credit, technologies, and equal participation in the labour force and in decision-making at all levels. They acknowledged that fertility control is the basis for enjoyment of other rights and called for universal family planning services and special attention to the needs of adolescents. The strategies were addressed to governments, the international community, and NGOs. Progress on this framework for action is to be reported to the next international women's conference (Beijing, September 1995).

Meanwhile, many of the Nairobi proposals have been picked up, strengthened, and made more specific by United Nations bodies and NGOs at both policy and programme levels. The World Conservation Union (IUCN), after years of neglect, has established both a population programme and a women's programme, now under the general umbrella of a social policy service. Several donor agencies have incorporated women's issues and gender analysis into their development aid portfolios. In the non-governmental community, numerous workshops and local initiatives have provided platforms for women at various levels of society, especially in developing countries, to express their views and needs. There are small-scale success stories in all parts of the world, for example, those initiated by the Chipko Movement in India, the Green Belt Movement in Kenya, and Development Alternatives for Women in a New Era (DAWN).

In the run-up to the United Nations Conference on Environment and Development (UNCED), held in Rio de Janeiro in June 1992, strenuous efforts were made to get women, family planning, and population back on the environment agenda. Controversy still surrounded the last two, although the UNCED secretariat included advisors on both population and women. The very fact that there was opposition to population issues in general, at first from the Group of 77, and to family planning in particular from the Vatican, only served to heighten the attention given to these issues at the conference (Lassonde and Rowley 1992).

Many governments carried a strong family planning message to Rio. Addressing a meeting of the United Nations Association, Baroness Lynda Chalker, British Minister for Overseas Development, said: 'Women want us to listen to them as we plan development programmes on their behalf. They want to contribute—and to do this they need fuller and better information about health and family planning issues ... we expect the British aid programme to support an integrated approach to women's health and population. This is a central feature of our attempts to bring about sustained reductions in poverty' (Chalker 1992).

The UNCED conference stated, among its principles, that 'women have a vital role in environmental management and development. Their full participation is therefore essential to achieve sustainable development' (United Nations 1992*a*). Its recommendations are set out in a chapter on 'Global action for women towards sustainable and equitable development' and can be summarized as follows:

- all countries should implement the Nairobi forward-looking strategies for women which emphasize the need for women to participate in ecosystem management and control of environmental degradation;
- policies are needed to increase the proportion of women in pro- grammes for sustainable development involving decision- making, planning, and technical and management roles, and women's bureaux and non-governmental organizations must be strengthened;
- consideration should be given to issuing, by the year 2000, a strategy for eliminating constitutional, legal, administrative, cultural, behavioural, social, and economic obstacles to women's full participation in sustainable development and public life;
- by 1995, there should be national, regional, and international mechanisms to assess the impact of development and environ- ment programmes on women and ensure that they participate and benefit;
- educational policies and curricula should disseminate gender- relevant knowledge and promote the enhanced value of women's roles;
- priority measures are needed to eliminate female illiteracy, assure girls' universal access to primary and secondary education, expand enrolment in schools, and provide increased post- secondary training opportunities for women in the sciences and technology;
- there is a need to reduce the heavy workload of women and girls; governments, local authorities, and employers should establish affordable nurseries and kindergartens; and national pro- grammes are required to encourage men to share household tasks equally with women;
- environmentally sound technologies developed in consultation with women should be promoted and access provided to clean water, adequate sanitation facilities, and efficient fuel supplies;
- health facilities — including safe and effective woman-centred and woman-managed reproductive health care and family

planning services — should be strengthened and made more accessible, and comprehensive health care should include prenatal care, and information on maternal and child health and responsible parenthood, and should provide mothers the opportunity to breast-feed their infants for at least the first 4 months of life;

• women have a crucial role to play in changing unsustainable patterns of consumption and production, particularly in industrialized countries, and programmes are needed to develop consumer awareness and encourage investment in environmentally sound productive activities;

• countries should avert the rapid environmental and economic degradation in developing countries that generally affects women and children in rural areas, where major problems include drought, desertification, armed hostilities, natural disasters, toxic waste, and unsuitable agrochemical products;

• gender-impact analysis should be an essential component in programmes, and rural and urban training and resource centres are needed to disseminate environmentally sound technologies to women.

In May 1992 another important contribution to the formulation of international strategies was provided by a Technical Discussion on Women, Health and Development convened by the World Health Assembly. Among its proposals for action were the following (WHO 1992*b*):

If women are to realize their full potential in their productive roles, they must be able to manage their reproductive role. This means that they must have access to family planning information and services. These are essential if women's reproductive rights are to be secured. Moreover, practices carried out without women's informed consent should be identified and eliminated. The ability to decide freely and in an informed manner the number and spacing of one's children is the first step to enabling women to exercise other choices. When a woman realizes that she can make decisions regarding her reproductive function, this experience of autonomy spreads to other aspects of her life. It enables her to pursue diverse opportunities and empowers her to make pivotal decisions in her own life. Family planning is an essential means of enhancing women's autonomy.

Formal and non-formal education programmes should take into consideration value systems that discriminate against women. This includes customs and traditions that are often tolerated in many societies, but which are responsible for perpetuating inequities between men and women.

Donor and recipient countries are urged to adopt policies on women in development in order to ensure women have a more equitable share in access to resources and benefits, and to improve the developmental effectiveness of aid programmes. Such policies would be based on acknow-ledgement of the significant contribution that women make to national economies. These policies should apply to all aid activities in an effort to redress the unequal distribution of benefits of past aid programmes.

Endorsement of these concerns has also come from the World Conference on Human Rights, which took place in Austria in June 1993:

The full and equal participation of women in the political, civil, economic, social and cultural life at national, regional and international levels and the eradication of all forms of discrimination on grounds of sex are priority objectives of the international community ... the World Conference recognizes ... woman's right to accessible and adequate health care and the widest range of family planning services as well as equal access to education at all levels.

Priorities for action

Are all these pronouncements mere lip service? Why has there been so little progress on the status of women? Why are so many millions of women still out of reach of family planning and health care? Some of the answers have already been given in the foregoing discus-sion of women's roles and the obstacles that stand in the way of their advancement.

There are many reasons why action by governments on the agreed international strategies is so lethargic. Governments of developing countries are caught in the burden of debt, structural adjustment, and economic recession. Military expenditure still claims a dispro-portionate share of national budgets, with consequent neglect of even the most basic measures known to be prerequisites of sus-tainable development. Development agencies, although ostensibly behind the strategies their governments have endorsed, are fre-quently ambivalent in their policies for economic growth, human development, and resource management. Above all, there is the failure to focus on the gender issue as a critical variable, requiring urgent attention. Resources are not allocated to deal with that issue.

I believe, first, that a new ethical framework for action is needed. Such a framework must recognize that people are the primary resource for development. In this ethical framework, women and their needs should be the central focus. Throughout the world, it is women who bear the greatest burdens of physical labour, in both their productive and reproductive roles.

How can development take place when half the population suffers social, educational, and economic discrimination, is over-worked, under-nourished, illiterate, and constantly at risk of unwanted pregnancies? How can families be healthy and productive when women suffer severe risks that are associated with pregnancy and childbearing? It is a global disgrace that in today's world half a million women die each year due to pregnancy-related causes. It is totally unacceptable that young girls are married off before their bodies are prepared for motherhood. How can development take place when women have no control or choice over their own lives? Family planning can give women the choice and the chance to take some control. We must give women the choice.

Our ethical framework must recognize that people are the primary resource for development, but that the quality of their lives, thus their ability to participate fully, necessitates bringing their numbers into balance with the Earth's finite resources. Development begins with the participation of people. Sustainable development must take its energy from the experience and ability of those it aims to serve. Their knowledge of natural systems, local needs, and aspirations must be part and parcel of development strategies. Responding to their needs and aspirations is the first step, building on their knowledge and experience is the second.

Development, as conceived and managed in the past, has often failed to build on people's felt and expressed needs. It has been geared to economic growth rates, GNP, and economic productivity rather than to the simultaneous empowerment and participation of people, especially the women. We arrogantly assumed that we could give development to the unlucky poverty-stricken masses, ignoring people's knowledge, skills, and aspirations.

There are few societies in the contemporary world where women's special creativities and energies in shaping caring public policies in such areas as reproductive health, children, the youth, the elderly, and the environment are given a real chance. This is sad because women are considered to have more social imagination and commitment than men, and women are more willing to promote far-sighted solutions with their incumbent short-term sacrifices than men, who generally tend towards short-sighted expediency.

Health-care budgets are inadequate everywhere and need desperately to be increased; currently available funds are often poorly allocated, weighted toward curative rather than preventive measures. But real improvements in women's health status will require far-reaching socio-economic and cultural change extending beyond the health-care system. Because women's health is a direct reflection of their status, no strategy can be successful in the long term unless women become equal partners in social development. Systematic and fundamental changes in the nature of policies toward, and allocation of resources to, women will have to be addressed as part of a long-term strategy of change (World Bank 1992).

Efforts to expand family planning programmes have contributed to significant progress; the rate of contraceptive use in developing countries rose from 40 per cent in 1980 to 49 per cent in 1990 and 51 per cent in 1992. But the rate needs to increase by another 7 percentage points by 2000 and by yet another 5 percentage points by 2010. Unmet demand for contraceptives is large—it ranges from about 15 per cent of couples in Brazil, Colombia, Indonesia, and Sri Lanka to more than 35 per cent in Bolivia, Ghana, Kenya, and Togo. Meeting this demand is essential for reaching even the base case projections of the United Nations and will require that total annual expenditure on family planning increase from about $US5 billion to about $US8 billion (in 1990 prices) by 2000. An additional $US3 billion would be required to achieve a scenario of rapid fertility decline. Choices about family planning and education policies today will determine world population levels, and the consequent pressures on the environment, in the twentieth-first century.

It would be a gross neglect of our responsibilities if we do not hand over to the next millennium a world in which each and every woman in every corner of the globe has been informed about, and given the means to use, family planning. By the year 2000 we must dramatically increase the prevalence of contraceptive use if we really want a sustainable balance between population and resources to emerge in the next century.

At present only 1 per cent of development assistance goes into family planning programmes, about $US1 billion annually. Total spending on family planning from in-country and international sources needs to double in the next few years and reach at least $US4 billion by the end of the century. More resources, both national and donor, also need to be channelled to health and education sectors. Developing countries must themselves be prepared to change their priorities and make greater investments in health and family planning services and in the provision of adequate educational opportunities for all their citizens. A genuine partnership between donor agencies and governments is needed. The role of the private sector, especially the low-cost services of non-governmental organizations, should be expanded.

Finally, the human right to the knowledge of, and access to, family planning has been proclaimed by the international community. Yet at the political level, population and family planning continues—mysteriously—to be a hot potato in many countries.

Access to family planning remains hostage to governments' unwillingness to invest adequately in reproductive health services. Yet family planning is the essential prerequisite to unleashing the development potential of women. If energy, land, and water are the keys to survival, the keys are held by women.

REFERENCES

Brown, L. R. (1993). Food output has stopped keeping up. *International Herald Tribune*, July 1993, Paris.

Central Television (1992). The population issue. *Moving Pictures Bulletin, Special Issue on Population*. Central Television Enterprises, London.

Chalker, Baroness L. (1992). *People and their environment: preserving the balance*. Overseas Development Administration, London.

Davidson, J. and Dankelman, I. (1988). *Women and environment in the Third World: alliance for the future*. Earthscan, London.

Edstrom, J. (1992). Indicators for women's health in developing countries: what they reveal and conceal. *IDS Bulletin*, **123**, 38–49.

Fathalla, M. F. (1992). Reproductive health in the world: two decades of progress and the challenge ahead. *International Conference on Population and Development, Expert Meeting on Population and Women, June 1992*. United Nations Population Division, New York.

Harrison, P. (1992). *The Third Revolution: environment, population and a sustainable world*. I. B. Tauris/Penguin Books, London.

International Fund for Agricultural Development (1992). *The state of world rural poverty*. New York City University and Intermediate Technology Publications, New York.

Jacobson, J. L. (1992). *Gender bias: roadblock to sustainable development*. Paper No. 110. Worldwatch Institute, Washington DC.

Koblinsky, M. A., Timyan, J., and Gay, J. (ed.) (1992). *Women's health at the crossroads*. Population, Health and Nutrition Division, Population and Human Resources Department, World Bank, Washington.

Lassonde, L. and Rowley, J. (1992). Population: an emerging factor. In *Rio Reviews*. Centre for Our Common Future, Geneva.

Planet 21 (1993). Water for life. *People and the Planet*, **2**, (2). Planet 21, London.

United Nations (1972). *Conference on the human environment, Stockholm 5–16 June 1972*. United Nations, New York.

United Nations (1985). *Forward-looking strategies for the advancement of women*. Report of the World Conference to Review and Appraise the Achievements of the United Nations Decade for Women: Equality, Development and Peace. United Nations, New York.

United Nations (1992). *Report of the United Nations Conference on Environment and Development, Rio de Janeiro, 3–14 June 1992*, Vol. III, Chapter 24. United Nations, New York.

United Nations (1993). *World conference on human rights: the Vienna declaration and programme of action 1993*. UN Department of Public Information, New York.

United Nations Population Fund (UNFPA) (1991). *The state of world population 1991*. United Nations Population Fund, New York.

United Nations Population Fund (UNFPA) (1992). *The state of world population 1992*. United Nations Population Fund, New York.

United Nations Population Fund (UNFPA) (1993*a*). *Population issues*. Briefing Kit. United Nations Population Fund, New York.

United Nations Population Fund (UNFPA) (1993*b*). *The state of world population 1993*. United Nations Population Fund, New York.

World Bank (1992*a*). *Acting to save women's lives*. Report of a meeting of partners for safe motherhood. Population, Health and Nutrition Division, World Bank, Washington.

World Bank (1992*b*). *Development and the environment. World development report*. Oxford University Press.

World Commission on Environment and Development (1987). *Our common future*. Oxford University Press.

World Conservation Union (IUCN) (1992). Protected areas and demographic change: planning for the future. *Workshop Report, IVth World Congress on National Parks and Protected Areas, Caracas, February 1992*. World Conservation Union, Gland, Switzerland.

World Fertility Survey (1984). *World Fertility Survey. Major findings and implications*. World Fertility Survey, London.

World Health Organization (1992*a*). *Women's perspective and participation in reproductive health*. Report of a joint WHO/FIGO Workshop. World Health Organization, Geneva.

World Health Organization (1992*b*). *Women, health and development*. Report of the 1992 Technical Discussion. World Health Organization, Geneva.

6

Population and birth control: an Anglican perspective

Richard Harries

The Rt. Revd Richard Harries, Bishop of Oxford, was ordained in 1963 after Cambridge, theological college in Oxford, and a period in the Royal Corps of Signals. He served as a Curate in Hampstead until 1969 when he was appointed to a lectureship at Wells Theological College. In 1972 he became Vicar of All Saints, Fulham, and began to establish his considerable reputation as a broadcaster with his contributions to 'Prayer for the Day' on the BBC's Today programme. He left Fulham in 1981 to take up a new appointment as Dean of King's College, London. In 1987 he was appointed Bishop of Oxford.

Richard Harries has played a consistently active part in public debates on current issues, political as well as spiritual. He has written and spoken on questions of arms control and nuclear deterrence, and he is a leading authority on inter-faith, particularly Jewish–Christian, relations. He is the author of a number of books and articles on religious and international affairs.

WHY THERE IS A PROBLEM

It is not my task to deal in detail with the predicted figures for world population growth. Nevertheless, I need to set them out again very briefly in order to indicate the challenge with which we are faced. The figures suggest that over the next ten years there could be an annual increase in world population of up to 97 million. This is the equivalent of one United Kingdom every 7 months, or two whole Europes, east and west, over 10 years, or a school class of 30 every 10 seconds. Global population which today stands at about 5.6 billion could, on these predictions, be at least 10 billion by the year 2050, and on the worst case scenario, 12.5 billion, more than double what we are today. The bulk of this growth (97 per cent) will take place in the developing world. By the year 2025 the population of the developed world will form only 18 per cent of total world population, well below the 30 per cent it once was. These figures also reflect dramatic age differences. Before long, in the United Kingdom pensioners will outnumber young people. The developing world, however, will be predominantly young. As has been written (McRae 1993):

Imagine a Europe that feels like Bournemouth — a lot of older people, most quite comfortably off, with inevitably, the attitudes and values of that age and income group. Imagine an Africa that feels like the outskirts of Cairo — one that has become much more urban, and younger, sadly perhaps even poorer, and able to watch a soap opera version of the rich world through satellite television on every street corner.

Clearly, there are factors that would reduce those figures. AIDS is one feature of the future, for example. It has been estimated that in some countries as many as one-third of pregnant mothers are infected with the HIV virus (Anderson 1992). There is also the relative success of some countries in bringing down their rate of population growth. India now has a fertility rate of about four, a fall of about a third in the past 2 decades. China, after its ferocious policy of curbing family size, has a rate of about 2.4. Policies there and in other countries could become even more effective, making the present dire predictions look too pessimistic.

This rate of world population growth is seen as a major problem for a number of different reasons, which I will not go into. Stress has been laid recently upon the mass migrations which will result from it. Some emphasize the potential political instability. The two most often cited reasons, however, are the utilization of limited resources and damage to the environment. But on both these concerns we need to look first at the beam in our own eye before we focus on the mote in the eye of the developing world. For it is the developed world, forming only a minority of the world's population, that uses up most resources per head. A Bangladeshi, for example, consumes energy equivalent to three barrels of oil a year, a US citizen the equivalent of 55 barrels. The average person in Britain eats 12 000–14 000 calories of food equivalent a day, once animal feedstuffs are taken into account. The average food equivalent in India is only 3000 calories a day, less than a quarter of the British total.

Until now the developed, industrial world has certainly been the biggest culprit as far as the pollution of the environment and damage to the atmosphere is concerned. A family in the United States with only two children will consume more of the world's resources and produce more global pollution than a family in sub-Saharan Africa with over 30 children, were such a family to exist.

So it goes without saying that creating sustainable patterns of consumption in the North, which do minimal damage to the environment and atmosphere and which use up the minimum of resources, is the first challenge with which we are faced. If the major problems caused by world population growth are using up the world's resources and damaging the environment, then we in the developed world are very much part of those problems. That said, however, and that challenge faced, there are still good reasons why we should be concerned about population growth in the developing world. The first and most important reason is that countries with slower population growth rates saw annual incomes rise by an average of 1.23 per cent a year in the 1980s compared with a fall of 1.25 per cent in countries where population grew faster. Food production fell behind population growth in 67 out of 102 developing countries between 1978 and 1987. Population growth is integrally related to taking people out of poverty. And, with 1 billion people in the world living at or below starvation level, we do not need to be reminded of the urgency of this.

Secondly, as far as the environment and atmosphere are concerned, whereas the developed countries probably possess the capital and scientific resources to become environmentally clean by early next century, the atmospheric effects of such virtue are likely to be eclipsed by the continued increase in pollutants from China, India, Mexico, and other fast-industrializing countries now unable to afford sophisticated emission controls. The greenhouse effect, pollution of the seas, and the destruction of the forests affect us all, wherever the damage is being done.

So anxiety about the rate of world population growth is not just a selfish concern of the developed world. It vitally affects the living standards of the poorest countries themselves and it affects the quality of life of the whole globe.

ECONOMIC DEVELOPMENT OR FAMILY PLANNING?

Not everyone accepts this conclusion. There is a fundamental challenge both to the prophets of doom and to those who emphasize the necessity of national birth control programmes. This challenge comes, in different ways, from both the political right and the political left. An editorial in the Far-Eastern Economic Review (13 May 1993), was, for example, headed 'The more the merrier – reject the dismal prophets of population control'. This article drew a distinction between population and population density in Asia. It argued that population density is more significant than total population and that, interestingly, the places at the high end of the population density list are among the wealthiest in Asia – Hong

Kong, Singapore, Taiwan, South Korea, and Japan. Nor is this relationship confined to Asia. The Netherlands is one of the most crowded places on Earth but, the editorial said, 'We don't hear the World Bank warning of too many Dutchmen.' Indeed, the article suggested that there is often a racial cast behind the warnings of impending doom: 'The problem it seems, is always brown or yellow babies, never white ones.' More positively, it went on to argue that the best answer for those worried about population growth is economic prosperity. As people grow more wealthy, they tend to defer marriage and children; lower population rates follow rather than precede development. The solution it advocated, not surprisingly, was the opening of markets and the bringing about of a more effective capitalism.

From the Left and also the Roman Catholic Church a similar message comes: concentrate on development (though there is less emphasis here upon the benign effects of capitalism). Development agencies have for decades now urged that the fundamental problem is lack of development, exacerbated by the burden of Third World debt, unfair terms of trade, and so on. They, too, have argued that if only people can be given adequate food, housing, health, and education the rate of population growth will inevitably fall, for a variety of reasons, not least because infant mortality will fall and it will not be necessary to have a dozen children in order to ensure that two of them stay alive to keep their parents in their old age. In short, what we have here is a justice problem; and an undue emphasis upon family planning can detract from this. Not surprisingly, it is the developmental, justice aspect of world population growth which is emphasized by the Roman Catholic Church. It is a view with which the Anglican Church has much sympathy. This is of course a disputed area, but the evidence suggests that however much we, quite properly, stress the necessity of economic development, family planning still has an important role to play. Bangladesh is one of the world's poorest and most densely populated countries yet fertility rates declined by 2 per cent between 1970 and 1991, to 5.5 children per woman from 7. In that period contraception use among married women of reproductive age rose from 3 per cent to 40 per cent. Evidence from the world fertility survey suggests that if all women in the developing world who do not wish to become pregnant were empowered to exercise that choice, then the rate of population growth would fall by about 30 per cent. By the year 2025 this could translate into 3 billion fewer people. It seems clear that economic growth and the availability of family planning need to go together. As Mauldin and Sinding (1993) have written:

At times there has been controversy as to whether socio-economic development or family planning is more important. We believe that this has become
a largely academic question, as research has shown over and over again that
both contribute to declining fertility, and that the more of each is present
the faster fertility will decline. Socio-economic development is clearly the
more important factor because it sets the parameters within which programmes function; however, no matter how rapid socio-economic development is, the transition from high to low fertility is greatly aided by well
organised family planning programmes, as the last decade has clearly
demonstrated.

No organization could be more committed to social justice and
sustainable development than Oxfam. Yet they fully support the
availability of birth planning services because there is an expressed
and unmet need for them, especially among women. Such services
contribute to improving the health of women, especially in the reduction of maternal mortality. For example, 150 000 women a year die
through illegal abortions. Birth planning services help to improve the
well-being of children and they increase opportunities for women's
personal and social development.

Some recent evidence shows that the traditional assumption that
family size falls with economic progress does not always hold true.
Sri Lanka, Thailand, Bulgaria, and Kerala in India have all shown
sharp falls in family size despite relatively low prosperity, while the
Gulf States have maintained fertility rates of more than three during
a period of sharply rising wealth. As David Coleman (1993) has said:
'The things that really bring down family size are more complex, to
do with culture and education.' Kerala is a good example. Unlike the
rest of India there is a 90 per cent literacy rate, a high percentage
of Christians and the Communist party has been in power for significant periods.

The reasons that Oxfam puts forward to support the availability
of family planning services, as part of its total commitment to
development, point to the heart of the matter. It emphasizes
availability of choice for parents, particularly women. The opportunity to exercise responsible parenthood, to choose the number of
children to have and when to have them in order that the possibilities
for their well-being and development might be maximized, is the key
consideration. It is the key consideration in both the developed and
the developing world. It is the crucial factor whether or not there
is a challenge posed by predictions of dramatic growth in the world's
population.

THE ANGLICAN ACCEPTANCE OF CONTRACEPTION

Before I go on to say something more specific about Anglican approaches I should stress that I will be dealing simply with the issue of contraception. I will not be discussing sterilization directly, nor abortion, to which the Church of England is strongly opposed, except in the most carefully defined circumstances.

From an Anglican perspective birth *control* is unacceptable. It smacks too much of coercion and the developed world telling the developing one what to do. Birth control is out but birth *choice* is in. Indeed, as has been argued elsewhere, 'demographic targets that governments set can in most cases be met or exceeded simply by responding to the *expressed reproductive goals* of individuals. Family planning objectives should be expressed in terms of satisfying *'unmet need'* [for contraceptive provision]' (Sinding 1992).

The availability of contraception enlarges the area of our choice and offers greater opportunity for us to take responsibility for our own lives and those of our offspring, with a view to their well-being and growth under God. From this standpoint the Anglican Church fully supports making the information and technology as widely available as possible. Understandably, however, the Church of England had to move from an inherited position of opposition. The Church of England as such has made no independent contribution to this subject. Rather it has played its part in the formulations of successive Lambeth Conferences, the decanal gathering of Anglican Bishops from throughout the world. Resolution 41 of the 1908 Lambeth Conference (R. Coleman 1992) said

The Conference regards with alarm the growing practice of the artificial restriction of the family, and earnestly calls upon all Christian people to discountenance the use of all artificial means of restriction as demoralising to character and hostile to national welfare.

Resolution 68 of the 1920 Lambeth Conference revealed a shift away from absolutism. 'The Conference, while declining to lay down rules which will meet the needs of every abnormal case,' it began. However, it continued:

... regards with grave concern the spread in modern society of theories and practices hostile to the family. We utter an emphatic warning against the use of unnatural means for the avoidance of conception, together with the grave dangers — physical, moral and religious — thereby incurred, and against the evils with which the extension of such use threatens the race.

It went on to urge the importance of self-control and to assert that the primary purpose of marriage is the continuation of the race through the gift and heritage of children. The sexual union was not to be regarded as an end in itself.

Resolution 9 of the 1930 Conference showed a much more positive attitude. 'The functions of sex as a God-given factor in human life are essentially noble and creative.' And Resolution 13 began, 'The Conference emphasises the truth that the sexual instinct is a holy thing implanted by God in human nature.' In contrast to the 1920 Resolution it said that 'It acknowledges that intercourse between husband and wife as the consummation of marriage has a value of its own within that sacrament, and that thereby married love is enhanced and its character strengthened.' Resolution 15, voted on with 193 in favour and 67 against, said:

Where there is a clearly felt moral obligation to limit or avoid parenthood, the method must be decided on Christian principles. The primary and obvious method is complete abstinence from intercourse (as far as may be necessary) in a life of discipline and self-control lived in the power of the Holy Spirit. Nevertheless in those cases where there is such a clearly felt moral obligation to limit or avoid parenthood, and where there is a morally sound reason for avoiding complete abstinence, the Conference agrees that other methods may be used, providing that this is done in the light of the same Christian principles.

The 1958 Lambeth Conference was less qualified. Resolution 115 reads:

The Conference believes that the responsibility for deciding upon the number and frequency of children has been laid by God upon the consciences of parents everywhere: that this planning, in such ways as are mutually acceptable to husband and wife in Christian conscience, is a right and important factor in Christian family life and should be the result of positive choice before God.

In 1968 Resolution 22 noted the publication of the Papal Encyclical, *Humanae Vitae* and, while expressing its appreciation of the Pope's deep concern for the institution of marriage and the integrity of married life, went on:

Nevertheless, the Conference finds itself unable to agree with the Pope's conclusion that all methods of conception control other than abstinence from sexual intercourse or its confinement to the periods of infecundity are contrary to the 'order established by God'. It affirms the resolutions of the 1958 Conference of 113 and 115.

These resolutions show clearly how the Lambeth Conference

moved from total opposition, to qualified acceptance, and then full acceptance. My predecessor, Kenneth Kirk, who was Bishop of Oxford from 1937 to 1955, was previously Regius Professor of Moral and Pastoral Theology in Oxford. In a book first published in 1927 but revised for a new edition in 1936 he suggested that the main two reasons for a change in the attitude of the Anglican Church were, first, enhanced appreciation of the value of children, with the implied assumption that it might be easier to express this value if there are fewer rather than more. Secondly, and this is the main reason he gives, the change in the position of women. This, he wrote, 'has led to a natural, proper and wholly Christian demand that the wife should not be forced, by the exigencies of married life, to abandon all the activities in which she found her interests and occupation before marriage'.

All the recent Anglican statements on this subject have set contraception firmly within the context of a loving, stable, and life-long marriage union. It is the importance of this above all that has been stressed. As part of this, as was seen from the changing emphasis in the Lambeth Conference resolutions, there has been a growing appreciation of the value of the marital sexual union in itself, for itself. This change can be particularly clearly seen in the introduction to the marriage service. The 1662 Book of Common Prayer stated that the causes for which matrimony was ordained were:

First, it was ordained for the procreation of children, to be brought up in the fear and nurture of the Lord, and to the praise of his holy name. Secondly, it was ordained for a remedy against sin, and to avoid fornication, that such persons as have not the gift of continency might marry, and keep themselves undefiled members of Christ's body. Thirdly, it was ordained for the mutual society, help, and comfort that the one ought to have of the other, both in prosperity and adversity.

The 1928 Book kept the first reason, though in slightly different language. The language of the second reason, however, was changed radically.

Marriage was ordained that the natural instincts and affections, implanted by God, should be hallowed and directed aright; that those who are called of God to this holy estate, should continue therein in pureness of living.

The Alternative Service Book of 1980 has a totally rewritten introduction. It gives the reasons for marriage in these words:

Marriage is given, that husband and wife may comfort and help each other, living faithfully together in need and in plenty, in sorrow and in joy. It is given, that with delight and tenderness they may know each other in love, and through the joy of their bodily union, may strengthen the union of their hearts and lives. It is given, that they may have children and be blessed in caring for them and bringing them up in accordance with God's will, to his praise and glory.

Here we see that what was traditionally the third reason, mutual society, help, and comfort, has become the first reason. The second reason, relating to the sexual instinct, has become very positive, its purpose 'that with delight and tenderness they may know each other in love', whereas the traditional first reason, the procreation of children, has become the third one.

Professor Gordon Dunstan, one of Anglicanism's foremost ethicists in recent years, reflecting on the process whereby the Anglican Church changed its mind on this issue, has written that the resolutions did no more than reflect 'a moral judgement already made, tested and acted upon by Christian husbands and wives, episcopal and clerical as well as lay, for years before' (Dunstan 1974). He went on to say that:

It exemplifies an instance in which the *magisterium* of the Church formulated and ratified a moral judgement made by a sort of *Consensus Fidelium*, for which a good theological justification was worked out *ex post facto*. That *Consensus* which, in the history of doctrine, has been claimed as the forerunner of dogmatic formulation, is here claimed as a source of moral insight which a church may, indeed must after testing, properly make its own.

This is a crucial indication of the nature of Anglican moral judgements. They are not simply laid down from on high. The official pronouncements of the Church reflect the tested experience of the wider Christian community, particularly that of lay people. Another good example of change, though one which took rather longer to effect, would be the way the Church, after more than 1000 years' fierce condemnation of usury, accepted that lending money on interest for the purposes of trade was morally legitimate.

ROMAN CATHOLIC ARGUMENTS

For several decades now there has been no Anglican voice arguing against contraception. The main arguments against have come from the official pronouncements of the Roman Catholic Church. With some temerity I must now consider these. I hesitate to do so because we are so used these days to working together in mutual charity and forbearance, refraining from criticism of one another. Nevertheless, there is a clear difference here, which must be honestly stated.

Perhaps it is legitimate to do so because, as is well known, there is fierce disagreement within the Roman Catholic Church itself. The Papal Commission set up by Pope John XXIII on this issue produced a majority report which allowed for the moral legitimacy of artificial means of contraception. Much to the shock of many of the faithful, Pope Paul VI took a different line in *Humanae Vitae*, firmly upholding the traditional prohibition. Since then, however, debate has continued unabated, with many reputable Roman Catholic theologians opposing the Papal line. However, it has its defenders. A major work by an American Professor of Philosophy, Janet Smith, published in 1991, surveys *Humanae Vitae*, 'a generation later' and in some 425 pages defends both its conclusions and reasoning. I have time to focus on only one kind of argument, that from natural law. The first key phrase of *Humanae Vitae* appears in paragraph 11. 'The Church ... in urging men to the observance of the precepts of the natural law ... teaches as absolutely required that in *any use whatever of marriage* there must be no impairment of its natural capacity to procreate human life.' The second key phrase occurs in paragraph 12: 'This particular doctrine ... is based on the inseparable connection, established by God, which man on his own initiative may not break, between the unitive significance and the procreative significance which are both inherent in the marriage act.'

The key phrase in paragraph 11 reads in the Italian, the language in which *Humanae Vitae* was written: '*Che qualsiasi atto matrimoniale dev e rimanere aperto alla transmissione della vita*' (see Smith 1991, p. 78). The Latin (the official language of the Church) substitutes the words *Per se destinatus* (in itself ordered) for the Italian *aperto* (open) although the Latin *apertus* would apparently easily have worked here. The phrase *Per se destinatus*, though, is philosophically more precise. One version of the Catholic Truth Society translation reads: 'It is absolutely required that any use whatever of marriage must *retain its natural potential* to procreate human life.' Another version renders this phrase rather freely but faithfully: 'In any use whatever of marriage there must be *no impairment of its natural capacity* to procreate human life.' Earlier criticisms of Papal teaching had often pointed out that we continuously interfere in nature for human well-being. Every medical operation is in some sense contrary to nature. Roman Catholic critics had therefore described the traditional natural law teaching, which suggested that the biological function gave the theological meaning, as biologism or physicalism. Janet Smith argues that a rational defence of the natural law objection to contraception does not depend on purely biological or physiological arguments. She thinks that contraception is wrong not simply because an act of sexual intercourse has its physiological end violated but because it is a *human* act of sexual intercourse and thus a violation of man not only in his physiological dimension but in his psychological and spiritual dimension as well. However, this said, she does nevertheless hold that this understanding of a human act is in some sense dependent upon the physiological significance of the act. This is how she states what she calls Version C of the Natural Law argument, which she finds to be fundamentally sound:

1. It is wrong to impede the procreative power of actions that are ordained by their nature to the generation of new human life.
2. Contraception impedes the procreative power of actions that are ordained by their nature to the generation of new human life.
3. Therefore, contraception is wrong.

When we look further at her argument her emphasis is on the fact that human life is a great good. Furthermore, 'human life is such a great good that not only should life itself be respected but so too should the actions that lead to the coming to be of human life' (Smith 1991, p. 101). She then gives the example of how we transfer respect from one thing to something else; for example, we extend the respect that we have for an individual to members of his or her family. But a couple may very well argue that they have the highest respect for human life and just because they have this respect they intend to plan carefully how many children they are going to have and when they are going to have them, in the most careful and scientific way possible. Or, we might argue, we have the highest respect for human life as a gift from God, and are quite willing to transfer this respect to the means by which life is generated. But it by no means follows that this respect precludes limiting, by technical means, the times when that life can be procreated.

Let me approach the matter from a different angle. The evolutionary significance of the act of intercourse is no doubt that children might be produced and the species flourish. But that may only rarely be the conscious motive of those who engage in the act. Similarly, experience shows that physical intercourse can nourish and bond the union between a man and his wife. But it is doubtful whether the couple engage in intercourse specifically for that purpose. Rather, they make love because they want to, it feels natural, it is a way of giving and receiving pleasure, and a way of drawing close to the other person. If we are talking about the human meaning of the act, which it is surely right to do, then the human meaning transcends, though it can include, any of these three ways of looking at it. A couple can consciously hope to conceive. They can consciously hope that their union will be deepened. They can consciously hope that they will give and receive pleasure. But the conscious, human, meaning is not to be identified with any biological reason why the couple come together.

Paragraph 12 of *Humanae Vitae*, already quoted, says that there is an inseparable connection, which man may not break, 'between the unitive significance and the procreative significance which are both inherent to the marriage act'. Janet Smith seems weak on arguments to support this, maybe because there are none that really stand up. I would say: A kitchen table may be designed for eating, but writing letters on it is a perfectly acceptable and proper use. Or, to take an analogy she sometimes uses, that of the eye, she suggests that the purpose of the act of intercourse is to produce children as the purpose of the eye is to see. But the eye itself is a means whereby impressions are registered on the brain. The human act of seeing goes way beyond the recording of impressions. It includes reflection, association, and imagination. It produces great works of art and can lead into delight and praise. No doubt evolution produced the eye in order to help us survive. But survival is rarely to the forefront of our seeing. The act of seeing becomes a human act of seeing involving the mind and heart and soul. While it is true that the human act remains dependent upon a physiological process, the meaning of that act is certainly not so dependent. Similarly, the act of intercourse remains dependent upon certain physiological happenings. But the meaning is a human meaning that is not circumscribed by those physiological processes.

Anglicans would argue that one of the purposes of marriage, as indicated in all our prayer books, is the procreation of children. But this is a purpose that belongs to the whole marriage, and is not tied to every particular sexual act. Janet Smith considers this view under what she calls the 'principle of totality' (Smith 1991, p. 89 ft.). She argues that from a moral point of view each act must be considered individually and that they cannot receive their moral specification as part of the totality. She gives the following example.

Restaurant owners may be open on occasion to serving blacks, but on occasion not. Could they argue that the 'totality' of their acts are open to integration? They may also argue that the good of the restaurant requires such occasional discrimination, otherwise they would not get enough business to stay open. Moreover, staying open is in the best interests of the blacks whom they would like to integrate into the clientele of the restaurant. Some would argue that each act of discrimination is wrong, but the principle of totality, as understood by many theologians, would seem to justify acts of discrimination designed to serve the purpose of integration.

This, however, is a totally misleading analogy. Acts of discrimination are wrong in themselves. They cannot be made right by being seen as part of a total programme of integration. Acts of sexual intercourse which use contraceptive methods, however, are not wrong in themselves. They are, or can and ought to be, human acts expressive of love, nourishing the marriage bond. As already argued, this purpose can stand independently of the purpose of procreation.

Professor Gordon Dunstan points out that Resolution 115 of the 1958 Lambeth Conference: 'Affirms a duty — to subordinate procreation to responsible decision — and a liberty to choose such means to this end as conscience, in view of the particular circumstances of the marriage, shall decide' (Dunstan 1974). That well sums up the Anglican view, the duty to make a responsible decision and a liberty to choose appropriate means to this end.

I come back to a point made earlier, namely that earlier Lambeth Conferences did in fact reflect the experience of Christian people, Bishops, priests, and lay women and men. I believe that this will in the end be the case in the Roman Catholic Church. At an intellectual level, the debate shows no signs of diminishing (Mahoney 1987). The opposition continues despite repeated Papal reiterations of the traditional teaching. Meanwhile lay people have made their decision. Fertility rates in Western Europe now average only about 1.7 children per woman — the UK rate is 1.8, Italy and Spain have rates of only 1.2, below levels in former West Germany of 1.4. The figures of predominantly Catholic countries such as Italy and Spain speak for themselves. It is unlikely that this low rate of fertility is simply the result of the rhythm method. I believe that in due course Roman Catholic lay experience will be reflected in official Catholic teaching as, in the 1930s, Anglican lay experience began to influence declarations of successive Lambeth Conferences.

REFERENCES

Anderson, R. (1992). Address to the Royal Society of Physicians, London. Reported in *The Independent*, 13 May.

Coleman, D. (1993). Quoted by Bronwen Maddox in *The Independent*, 27 March.

Coleman, R. (1992). *Resolutions of the Twelve Lambeth Conferences, 1867–1988*. Anglican Book Centre, Toronto.

Dunstan, G. R. (1974). *The artifice of ethics*, p. 48. SCM, London.

Kirk, K. E. (1936). *Conscience and its problems*, p. 292. Longmans Green, London.

McRae, H. (1993). *The Independent*, 12 May.

Mahoney, J. (1987). *The making of moral theology*, Chapter 7. Clarendon Press, Oxford.

Mauldin, W. P. and Sinding, S. W. (1993). In *Population Council Research Division working papers*, No. 50.

Sinding, S. W. (1992). Getting to replacement — bridging the gap between individual rights and democratic goals. In *Family planning: meeting challenges, promoting choices* (ed. P. Senanayake, and Keinman) IPPF.

Smith, J. E. (1991). Humanae Vitae, *a generation later*. Catholic University of America Press, Washington DC.

7

Mankind: master of this creation but servant of the Creator

John Jukes

The Rt. Revd John Jukes OFM Conv. has been the Roman Catholic Auxiliary Bishop of Southwark and titular Bishop of Strathearn since 1980. After training in Rome, he entered the Franciscan Order and was ordained in 1952. He founded the Order's seminary in Anglesey and served as its Rector until 1959. He then served as a parish priest, in Manchester and London, for 10 years until his appointment to be lecturer in canon law and Vice-Principal at the Franciscan Study Centre in Canterbury. In 1979, Bishop Jukes was elected a Minister Provincial in the English Province and Area Bishop for the Deaneries of Kent. He is Chairman of the World of Work Committee of the Bishops' Conference of England and Wales.

The role of the Catholic Church in society is based upon two main factors. One is the conviction of the Church that it is charged with the duty of announcing the gospel of Jesus Christ to all peoples. From this duty flows the other factor. This is to respond to the needs of the people of the Earth. This response follows from the commission given by Christ to His followers to serve one's fellow human beings. In doing this the fulfilment of the prime command to love God above everything is achieved. These factors are interdependent, one illuminating the other. The gospel of Jesus Christ is rooted in the life and teaching of Jesus Christ. It will endure for all time. From the truth of God's purpose for the human race, which the gospel declares, follows a certain and secure base for reflection and decision on the right course of action and progression to be established in human affairs. The truth of the gospel gives a perennial validity, expressed in permanent principles, which is the basis of the Church's response to the variable social needs of the human race.

Among these permanent principles must be noted the following: the unique dignity of the human being in this creation; the obligation of love according to the gospel for all other human beings; the overcoming of sin which leads to oppression of the poor; the defence of the poor and oppressed; the rejection of injustice and greed; and acceptance that it is of God's will that material goods have a universal destination. To these principles which clearly interact with the social organization of human beings and their daily lives must be added the principle of accepting that all human beings have a spiritual destiny.

The Catholic Church holds that it is commissioned by Jesus Christ to teach the truth about God and His purpose for the human race. This capacity starts by certifying as true that which the church has received from God by the process called Revelation. In addition the Church feels entitled and on occasions required to enunciate principles of the natural law, including principles of morality even in respect of the social order.[1] She exercises this right and duty when this is required by fundamental human rights or the salvation of souls. In speaking about questions of underdevelopment the present Pope has reminded us that his predecessor Pius VI noted that the Church does not have technical solutions as part of her remit from God. As a consequence the Church does not propose economic and political systems or programmes. Nor does she show preference for one or the other, provided that human dignity is properly respected and promoted. However, this does not mean that the Church has nothing to say on these matters. As an 'expert on humanity' the Church is duty bound to make proposals for the guidance of human behaviour which are in accord with true human dignity and the ultimate destiny of the human race.

The Catholic Church from her very beginning has never ceased from the declaration of the good news given her by Jesus Christ. The exploration of the consequence of the Son of God's coming into this world and the work of penetrating more deeply the mysteries of God have given an impetus present in every age for the growth of theological sciences. However, reflection upon the circumstances and needs of the human race in the context of the general call to eternal salvation has differed from age to age. The formulation and teaching of universal principles concerning human moral and social conduct has developed in a variety of levels of urgency and focus. Since the ending of the Second World War the Catholic Church has more and more focused her attention and teaching on matters which concern the economic, social, and environmental well-being of the human race. It is well known that a very large range of questions and issues of this type have received specific attention from the

---

[1] Code of Canon Law, 747, par. 2 relying upon a series of magisterial teaching documents: Pius XI, Enc. *Firmissimam Constantiam*, 28-3-1937; John XXIII, Enc. *Mater et Magistra*, 15-5-1961 and Enc. *Pacem in Terris*, 11-4-1963; IInd Vatican Council in CD 12, DH 15, GS 76, 89. Synod of Bishops: *Convenientes ex Universo*, 30-11-1971; John Paul II, *Sollicitudo Rei Socialis*, par. 41, 30-12-1987 and *Veritatis Splendor* par. 64, 6-8-1993.

teaching magisterium of the Church. Among these are the two topics which form the subject of this book, namely population matters and the environment.

It is part of the Catholic faith that Jesus Christ gave a special and distinctive duty to the Apostles He called and formed. This duty included a particular orientation to proclaiming the good news both in their own day and to the end of time. The Catholic Church believes that the duties entrusted to the Apostles by Christ have been transmitted to the college of bishops of the Catholic Church. In that college the Bishop of Rome, the Pope as successor of St Peter, has a unique and irreplaceable role. Thus on these issues of population and the environment the Pope and bishops have a special teaching role in the life of the Church in her service of humanity. This role is by no means exclusive of the true and authentic contribution to the Catholic position by many others in the Church. However, it is for the bishops with the Pope to declare if a teaching is authentically in conformity with the deposit of faith and the judgements made by the magisterium of the Church on moral principles or matters concerning the social order (John Paul II, *Veritatis Splendor*, par. 5). Thus it will be seen that the pronouncements of the Pope, either personally or through the organs of the Holy See, together with the formal teaching of bishops, either individually or in groups, have a distinctive and substantial role in presenting Catholic teaching on these issues.

The term 'Holy See' here is to be understood as the Pope teaching directly in writing or preaching, such as is found in Encyclical letters, Addresses, and other communications. It can also signify documents issued by the various departments of the Papal Curia which are intended to set out the Church's position on social questions. Since many of these questions are complex, often more than one department or Dicasteria of the Holy See is involved. In the case of questions to do with environment and population the Pontifical Councils for the Laity, for Justice and Peace, and for the Family are, with the Secretariat of State of His Holiness, very frequently involved.

It has been the custom of the Holy See to distinguish between questions which affect the environment and those which have to do with population. The starting point for any reflection on these topics is found in the Church's understanding of God's purpose in creating this universe and the manner by which the Creator brought human beings into it. However, from this common starting point specific principles appropriate to these topics individually are developed which are not necessarily common to each. It is useful here to recall what I have said above: the Church does not claim to be possessed of the capacity to offer technical solutions to the human situation. What is presented is an insight and reminder of the moral principles which must be adhered to in order that equitable and lasting solutions be found to the challenges confronting mankind.

The word 'environment' has a reminiscence for me of the Latin verb *vivo, vivere*, 'I live, to live'. In Latin *vivere* acts as a base for much more than simply indicating life or that something is living. It can mean to enjoy something, particularly the company of friends. Thus while for us environment indicates the space in which we live with all its complexities of both alive and inanimate beings, it may be that the Latin reminds us that it is we as living human beings who are the centre of this space. It is only very recently that global environmental questions have come to the fore in political and economic debate. Thus the teaching of the Holy See on the moral principles and issues respecting the global environment is recent. This teaching is, however, always centred upon human existence and final destiny.

The teaching of the Holy See on the moral aspects and principles of global environmental issues has its more recent roots in the response to questions on private ownership and the common good. Pope Leo XIII in his Encyclical letter *Rerum Novarum*, 15-5-1891, is often held to have opened the modern era of Catholic social teaching. In that letter Leo XIII was addressing the degraded condition of the working class in modern industrial society. He affirmed the duty of the State to intervene, where necessary, to regulate the excesses of individual owners of land and the means of production. At the same time he sustained the right to private ownership of goods, land, and services by individuals.

The Popes subsequent to Leo XIII have continued to study and refine the teaching upon the common good, state intervention, and the right of private ownership. The Second Vatican Council in the pastoral Constitution *Gaudium et Spes*, 7-12-1965, affirmed and developed this thinking (paras. 69 and 71). The most recent development of this teaching is found in the Encyclical letter *Centesimus Annus* issued by the present Pope on 5 May 1991. The fourth chapter of this letter is entitled: 'Private property and the universal destination of material goods'. The Pope explains this phrase, taken from *Gaudium et Spes*: 'Private property or some ownership of external goods affords each person the scope needed for personal and family autonomy, and should be regarded as an extension of human freedom ... Of its nature private property also has a social function which is based on the law of the common purpose of goods' (John Paul II, *Centesimus Annus*, 1-5-1991, par. 10).

Pope John Paul II goes on to examine the roots of this teaching. He states (John Paul II, *Centesimus Annus*, par. 31):

God gave the earth to the whole human race for the sustenance of all its members, without excluding or favouring anyone. This is the foundation of the universal destination of the earth's goods. The earth, by reason of its fruitfulness and its capacity to satisfy human needs, is God's first gift for the sustenance of human life. But the earth does not yield its fruits without a particular human response to God's gift, that is to say, without work. It is through work that man, using his intelligence and exercising his freedom, succeeds in dominating the earth and making it a fitting home. In this way, he makes part of the earth his own, precisely the part which he has acquired through work; this is the origin of individual property. Obviously, he also has the responsibility not to hinder others from having their own part of God's gift; indeed, he must cooperate with others so that together all can dominate the earth.

The Pope then proceeds to analyse the concrete economic and political realities of our times. He notes the ever-growing importance of the acquisition of personal skills in the modern world; the manner in which the modern business economy has grown; the immense disparity in wealth and opportunity for many members of the human family, especially in the Third World. He notes the claimed effectiveness of the free market for utilizing resources and effectively responding to needs. He emphasizes the duty of responding to certain human needs which the market is unable to meet.

The Pope focuses on the phenomenon of consumerism which can create lifestyles and attitudes which are obviously improper and often damaging to human physical and spiritual health. He teaches that while it is not wrong to live better, the pursuit of 'having' rather than 'being' puts the individual at risk of selfish exclusion of one's neighbour from the goods of the Earth that should be shared. It is here that the Pope sees the nub of the 'ecological question'. The Pope says (*Centesimus Annus*, par. 37–8):

In his desire to have and to enjoy rather than to be and to grow, man consumes the resources of the earth and his own life in an excessive and disordered way. At the root of the senseless destruction of the natural environment lies an anthropological error, which unfortunately is widespread in our day. Man, who discovers his capacity to transform, and in a certain sense create the world through his own work, forgets that this is always based on God's prior and original gift of the things that are ... Instead of carrying out his role as a cooperator with God in the work of creation, man sets himself up in place of God and thus ends up provoking a rebellion on the part of nature, which is more tyrannised than governed by him.

The Pope makes further reference to the destruction of what he calls the 'human environment' by which he means those circumstances of our times, such as unplanned urbanization, which seem to place grave obstacles to proper human social development.

Later in this chapter I will seek to present the theological principles from which the Pope and the Church have come to the conclusions concerning these environmental issues. I turn now to considerations of the Catholic Church's teaching on population matters. Here it should be noted that the Church holds that the first and fundamental structure for 'human ecology' is the family, in particular the ideal of the family founded on marriage.

The study of 'population' is a relatively recent addition to the behavioural sciences. With the keeping of accurate records of births and deaths the basic material became available for the work of sociologists to detect trends, to offer explanations, and, on occasions, to risk forecasts. Attempts to control the size of populations have long been part of the human story where nationalistic, political, or economic advantages were perceived by those who held power. More recently the success of technology and discoveries in the medical field have contributed to a large growth in populations in many parts of the world. This growth is often seen as the 'demographic problem' which poses a threat to the whole human race, if not in terms of the existence of our race then at least in regard to its well-being.

The Church's approach in this matter of population has always been from a starting point of the individual human being or family. This is not to say that the Church is ignorant of the challenge presented by the large increases in populations in many countries of the world, or indeed of the total world population. The Church, in her role as servant of mankind under God, cannot remain quiet in the face of challenges which touch upon the dignity and happiness of so many human beings. In meeting the challenge posed by the population question, the Church reminds all that the presence of human beings on this Earth is as a result of the Creator's specific purpose. From this position the Church employs her teaching and convictions about human beings to establish principles in the ethical order which will assist in arriving at a solution of the population issue.

Catholic teaching on human sexuality and reproduction is rooted in the vision offered in the Book of Genesis on the origin of creation and the human race. Human beings are made in the image and likeness of God (Gen. 1: 27). In the making of man God established the two sexes: 'male and female He created them'. He established their dominion over the Earth and required them to increase and multiply and so extend that dominion (Gen. 1: 28–30). The Catholic Church then affirms that human sexuality and reproduction are gifts of God and are therefore to be reverenced. The Church holds that the use of the sexual powers is ethically right only in the context of marriage. This conviction flows from the Genesis narrative, the teaching of Jesus on marriage and divorce (Matt. 19: 3–12), and the teachings of the Apostles, especially of Paul.

The Church holds that the family, whose basis is found in that lifelong commitment or covenant between a man and a woman which we call marriage, is the design of God in which the totality of conjugal love between a man and a woman can be fulfilled. Marriage then is not instituted by society or by some human agency for limited purposes of social control but is from God. (John Paul II, Apostolic Exhortation *Familiaris Consortio*, par. 11). Thus any proposals concerning the regulation of populations which ignore the family or make its existence and progress precarious are held by the Church to be ethically unjustified.

The Church has vigorously proclaimed the centrality of the family in God's plan for the continuance and perfection of the human race. In that proclamation two substantial questions have occupied the attention of the teaching authority of the Church. One is the question of direct intervention in the human reproductive process by way of contraception. The other is the development of the notion and practice of responsible parenthood. Both these questions warrant our close attention.

The Catholic Church with many other Christian Churches and denominations has always expressed her conviction of the wrongness of contraception.[2] This long and consistent tradition was not in itself seriously questioned until the second half of the twentieth century. Previous questioning had arisen from dualistic theories which had cast doubt upon the legitimacy of bringing new life into existence. However, the first half of the present century saw the establishment of a satisfactory understanding of the human female reproductive cycle. With this came the invention of a range of appliances and substances which either controlled fertility or aborted a fetus without surgical operation. Previously the prevention of fertilization of the ovum had involved some form of physical intervention in the act of copulation itself or its immediate consequences.

---

[2] There is a very substantial and constantly growing amount of writing among Roman Catholics on this issue. For a historical account of the consistant teaching on the immorality of contraception up to the twentieth century see Noonan (1965). For an extensive bibliography see Smith (1991), pp. 407–20.

These new inventions, which often seemed to avoid any form of such interventions, raised moral questions to which the pastors of the Church were called to respond.

This is not the occasion to describe at length the circumstances which led to the publication by Pope Paul VI of the Encyclical letter *Humanae Vitae*, 25-7-1968. The letter invoked an immediate reaction of hostility from a number of Catholics to one part of its teaching. This is the teaching which declared that 'the Church, which interprets natural law through its unchanging doctrine, reminds men and women that the teachings based on natural law must be obeyed and teaches that it is necessary that each conjugal act remain ordained in itself to the procreating of human life'.[3] In paragraph 14 of *Humanae Vitae* the Pope, as a consequence of this teaching by the Church, rejected the use of all forms of contraception which involved the direct interruption of the generative process already begun.

This teaching, which is logically at one with the unvarying tradition of the Church, has been maintained by the present Pope and in meetings of the Synod Bishops (see the Synod of Bishops, 28-10-80, and Pope John Paul II in *Familiaris Consortio*, 22-11-1981, par. 32). It is very significant for understanding the attitude of the Catholic Church on certain proposals for population control. Thus the Church feels obliged to oppose those methods which are aimed at directly intervening in the reproductive process. In one sense the Church is committed even more to opposing those systems of population control which involve direct and intended abortion or which use specific and purposely abortifacient substances. Such systems are a direct assault on innocent human life whose dignity is such that it lies outside human power to terminate.

It was and is most unfortunate that the contrary reaction to *Humanae Vitae*, which is particularly located in the richer and more economically developed countries of the world, has tended to obscure much of the teaching contained in *Humanae Vitae*. It must be emphasized that the Church's teaching on contraception is but a small part of the teaching on the dignity of the married state, the unitive and procreative element in marriage, and the central, indeed essential, role played by marriage and the family in the development of the social dimension of the human race.

One of the more obviously positive contributions to the teaching

---

[3] *Humanae Vitae*, par. 11. This is the translation by Janet E. Smith (1991) of the Latin: '*Ecclesia dum homines commonet de observandis praeceptis legis naturalis, quam constanti sua doctrina interpretatur, id docet necessariium esse, ut quilibet matrimonii usus ad vitam humanam procreandam per se destintus permaneat.*' See Smith (1991), note 7, pp. 78-9 and 281.

of the Church which has particular application to the topic of population is that of 'responsible parenthood'. A good description of this notion is found in the *Charter of the rights of the Family presented by the Holy See to all Persons, Institutions and Authorities concerned with the Mission of the Family in today's World*, 22-10-1983. Article 3 of the Charter includes the following:

The spouses have the inalienable right to found a family and to decide on the spacing of births and the number of children to be born, taking into full consideration their duties towards themselves, their children already born, the family and society, in a just hierarchy of values and in accordance with the objective moral order which excludes recourse to contraception, sterilization and abortion.

The convictions regarding responsible parenthood and the centrality of the family unit based on marriage have shaped the response of the Catholic Church at local, national, and international levels when questions of demography and population control have been debated in the public forum. Often the response of the Church to particular questions has been new, although always within the principles which have been outlined here. This is so because the questions themselves are new, arising out of new technologies or from a growth of awareness of the essential and growing social unity of the human race expressed in increased forms of economic and political interaction between individuals and nation states.

The Holy See has not been content to rest upon simply reiterating the principles on marriage, family rights, and man's place in creation. On the occasion of the 70th anniversary of the publication of *Rerum Novarum*, Pope John XXIII issued his encyclical letter, *Mater et Magistra*, 15-5-1961, which set out to survey the world-wide human social and economic scene. In this letter the Pope described the challenges facing the human race at the mid-point in the twentieth century, 1 year before the opening of the Second Vatican Council. In paragraphs 183 to 211 Pope John studied and defined the demographic and ecological challenge which was concerning many persons of good will. In subsequent paragraphs of the encyclical he proposed the basis of much of the teaching that has been outlined in this chapter and which has developed in subsequent papal teaching.

The Church, through the action of the Holy See, has been represented at, and has participated in, the 1974 and 1984 UN-promoted World Population Conferences. A continuous presence is maintained at the UN population division. On a number of occasions the Holy See has seen it necessary to protest over proposals to authorize and promote programmes of direct intervention by public authorities in the family's right and duty to exercise responsible parenthood. The Holy See has consistently promoted the growth of awareness needed for legitimate family planning and the necessity of proper economic development to establish an ecological balance so that the planet can properly support the human race for which it was made by God.

The Church welcomes, respects, and encourages the work and researches of scientists in the complex field of environmental and ecological studies. It is only when such work results in advice and policies which conflict with the vision of human dignity and God's purpose for the world that the Church is obliged to indicate her opposition. The Church, as has been stated before, does not understand her role to include a commission to offer technical solutions to the challenges presented in these matters.

I have conceived it to be my duty in this chapter simply to state the teaching of the Catholic Church which has reference to environmental and population matters. I have done this by relying upon teaching contained chiefly in papal documents in order to ensure that those who read this chapter will be left in no doubt as to the authenticity of what I have presented. I have not attempted to present any apology for, or justification of, this teaching. To do this would require much more space and time than is at my disposal. However, I do propose to present the final part of this chapter in the form of a personal reflection upon one of the principal sources of Catholic teaching, namely the initial chapters of the Book of Genesis. I do this in the hope that I can convey something of the majesty and blessing of God's design for the human race. I believe that this design, once accepted, gives hope and, indeed, a sure guide to the right way forward to those human beings who occupy themselves with these questions of the environment and population.

The first three chapters of the Book of Genesis are concerned with the basic creation event of our world by God and the place of mankind in that world. These chapters are a special form of narrative, setting out a form of religious writing about how things began and why they exist. The narrative is intent upon showing the power and majesty of God and His particular purpose for the human beings who come into being at the end of the creative process.

The Old Testament supports the Genesis creation narrative by showing God as the absolute Lord. This is expressed by the action of making all things out of nothing by the simple voice of command. There is no pre-existing matter; there is no constraint upon the Divine decision. All that God made is good because it is from God and is His to do with as He wills. Attempts which have been made to align the Genesis narrative of creation with the reflections and conclusion of modern cosmologists are not fruitful. It is simply not a scientific form of writing. However, this is not to say that it is not true, that it does not respond to reality. Despite what I have said above about the alignment of creation with the Genesis narrative, in listening to the Royal Institution Christmas Lectures 1993 by a prominent particle physicist, Professor Frank Close, I was fascinated to note that as he approached the climax of his lectures in the Big Bang theory of the origin of the universe, the majestic phrase from Genesis 'God said "Let there be light" and there was light' seemed a more than adequate way to express these theories. However, I insist that the reality conveyed in Genesis 1–3 is expressed in the general statement: all things have their ultimate origin in God and without God would not remain in being.

Genesis 1–3 contains two narratives of creation. Both coincide in showing the making of man as the culmination of the creative activity of God. The human being is made uniquely in the image and likeness of God; God is shown as breathing the breath of life into man, fashioned from the earth. Male and female as made by God possess the same nature. To both is given dominion over all living things. The human beings are required to be fruitful and to increase and fill the Earth. The narrative is shaped to show human dominion over living things by the action of naming all members of the animal kingdom by the man. This acts as an introduction to the special creation of the woman using the man's body and thus showing not simply equality between the man and the woman but also the union of complementarity between the sexes.

The Genesis narrative teaches that God's purpose for the human race included a gift of original happiness, together with a commission not simply to dominate but also to shape the Earth. This is what I understand to be the message contained in the device of being required to cultivate the garden of Eden. Under this command the man enjoyed freedom to use and enjoy both the initial gift of the garden and the work of his hands. However, attached to this munificence was one command: not to eat of the fruit of the tree of the knowledge of good and evil. This I understand to be a concrete way by which the human being was to recognize his own limitations and not to set himself up in competition to God. Thus man is not able to set up his own moral standards since he is a created being and so must derive these from God who alone gives being and freedom to be.

The Genesis narrative completes the presentation of the creation of our universe by telling of the Fall. The failure of Adam and Eve to obey the author of their existence brings about a substantial change in the relationship between the human race and the material creation. The simple and undisturbed exercise of dominion over nature becomes onerous and burdensome. The clear vision derived from the rational clarity of being made in the image and likeness of God is obscured. The balance in the individual human being of control of emotions and passions is gravely impaired. Suffering and death enter into the human experience. What is not lost is the continuing dominion over all nature. To this is added the promise of redemption and ultimate triumph over deception and sin.

These conclusions drawn from the Genesis narrative of creation give a basis for constructing what might be described as elements for a Catholic doctrinal and moral theology in respect of environment and population.

The environment is that physical inheritance given by God to mankind at the beginning of the human race. It comprises both inanimate and life forms. None of these is superior to man. All are at the service of the human race. No individual life form is superior to any individual human being. Man has the right, which is also a duty, to shape the environment. This is done by work. It is correct, then, to describe mankind as co-creator with God but within the limitations attached to a limited creature.

God gave to mankind the quality of dominion over the environment. This gift was not simply personal to Adam and Eve but one that is the patrimony of the human race throughout its history. Individual human beings exercise personal dominion and an activity of a limited creation in perfectioning the environment. However, this exercise of dominion has to respect the same basic right owned by all other human beings, both of the present generation and of the generations to come. There are then elements of both individual and universal ownership in the human relationship to the environment. Both these elements have to be kept in a balance of justice when disputes over the environment arise between individuals and between groups of human beings.

I maintain that the environment does not have rights of its own but only in relationship to human beings. When, therefore, man is spoken of as steward of the environment or of creation, this must be understood as referring to the individual human being's relationship to God and to other human beings. Man exercises stewardship of the environment under pressure of a native competitiveness. This burden follows from the Fall, whereby the balance of man's dominion over nature was disturbed and the relationships between human beings was impaired by sin. However, this disturbance, for the human being redeemed by Christ, is within his power to overcome under the influence of grace. His relationships with other human beings directed away from sin to God, provide the remedy for harmful competition.

It is of great significance that God sent His Son Jesus, the Redeemer, into this world, and in the course of achieving our redemption gave Him the opportunity to participate in the work of shaping the environment. Most of Jesus' life was spent in the ordinary round of human activity in Palestine. He was known as the carpenter of Nazareth (Mark 6: 3). This exercise of a skilled yet socially humble craft underlines the value to be placed upon operating in and shaping the environment. The redemption achieved by Jesus Christ extends to all creation for it is in our environment that our salvation has to be worked at in preparation for our fulfilment in the new heaven and earth.

The origin of the human race from a single pair is a powerful statement of the unity both in origin and in history of the human race. This is reinforced by the narrative of the Fall and the inheritance of punishment for sin, which is shown as extending to all human beings. Any studies or proposals which affect any human population have to take account of the essential solidarity of the human race. Our race is comprised of individuals made, each and everyone of. us, in the image and likeness of God. The use of the word 'image' indicates the general similarity of nature by reason of intellect and will, and a measure of authority between God and man (likeness is used to ensure that man is not made equal to God). Thus a human population is made of individuals who have a dignity which is rooted in a certain similarity with the Creator, the origin and necessary support in being of all creation.

The dignity of human beings, constituted by being made in the image and likeness of God, was marred but not destroyed by sin. The coming of the Son of God, the Eternal Word, to reverse the consequences of sin is a demonstration of God's intention to yet further elevate human nature and individual human beings to the divine. This elevation (which amongst Catholic theologians is called sanctifying grace) is available to all who freely accept the redemptive love of God. It is this potential for response to the divine gift of redemption, and hence for elevation to share with the divine life, which always has to influence any approach to population considerations and policies. Thus approaches and decisions made in the present time must not put human beings at risk with regard to their future eternal dignity. Policies and programmes which include elements which are unethical and immoral (such as abortion) need to be revised so as to exclude such elements.

It is clearly God's will expressed in the phrase 'Be fruitful, multiply, fill the earth and conquer it' that the human race is to continue. It is also clear that this process must be subject to the respect due to the moral law derived from the will of God. In discerning this moral law, the dignity of the individual and dimension of solidarity which must obtain between each individual human being are major elements. The detailed working out of tensions which are seen to arise over the growth of population and the limitation of resources of the Earth is the work of those who have responsibility and expertise in these fields. Yet in so doing there can be no hope of success unless the moral principles derived from God's will for the human race are observed.

Catholic theology in respect of the environment and population issues does not provide technical solutions. Yet it has an eminently practical application for measuring the ethical base necessary to ensure effectiveness of measures to deal with problems that arise in these fields of human concern. An example of how the Church feels able to contribute to the need to resolve these issues is found in the focus upon 'integral and sustainable development' which was the theme of the Encyclical letter of Pope Paul VI *Populorum Progressio*, 26-3-1967. The theme of this encyclical was taken up by Pope John Paul II in his Encyclical *Sollicitudo Rei Socialis*, 30-12-1987. The Popes noted that the search for solutions to the challenges presented by poverty and injustice in much of the world could be met by a commitment of all nations to developing the material resources of the world. Yet in that development the future of the human race should not be put in peril. Furthermore, development signified not simply material advance but a type of progress which respected the totality of the needs of human beings.

Both the environment and population are part of the human reality, yet not the whole of it. That reality is only complete when it is appreciated that the human race has been placed in this creation to crown and complete it and so fulfil the divine purpose. That purpose finds its ultimate fulfilment in being called to testify to the glory of God: the merciful, all-powerful Creator; the source of all being and perfection; the sustainer in being of all that is, or ever will be; the Hope, Delight, and Lover of man made in His image and likeness.

It is my hope that those who have participated in this book, together with all those who study questions related to the environment and population, accept that Catholic teaching, together with that of many other Christians, related to these matters is a rich resource of inspiration and hope for the success of their endeavours. I feel that there is always the danger that theology and religion, since it deals with that which is not immediately measurable or subject to testing, will be dismissed as untrue or at best irrelevant or impractical. I am reminded of the saying in the book of Proverbs: 'Where there is no vision the people perish' (Prov. 29: 8). May our experts and leaders be possessed of the vision that I have tried to convey.

ACKNOWLEDGEMENTS

I must acknowledge with deep gratitude materials supplied to me by Bishop James T. McHugh, Bishop of Camden NJ, USA, and Robert Whelan of the Committee on Population and the Economy.

REFERENCES

There are many references in the text to Encyclical letters and Aposotlic exhortations of the Popes. The English text of these documents is readily available from the Catholic Truth Society, c/o Ashley Place, London SW1P 1LT, UK; Tel. 0171 834 1363.

Noonan, J. T., Jr (1965). *Contraception*. Harvard University Press, Boston, Mass.
Smith, J. E. (1991). Humanae Vitae, *a generation later*. Catholic University of America Press.

8

Population, health, and environmental crises in the former Soviet Union[1]

Murray Feshbach

Professor Murray Feshbach is the world's leading expert on the demography, health, and ecology of the former Soviet Union. After graduating in history at Syracuse University, he took his Master's degree at Columbia University, New York and his Ph.D., in economics, at The American University. He worked for 25 years in the US Department of Commerce, eventually becoming Chief, USSR Population, Employment, and Research and Development Branch in the US Bureau of the Census. In 1986 Professor Feshbach, a fluent Russian speaker, became the first Sovietologist-in-residence in the Office of the Secretary-General of NATO, Lord Carrington. He is currently Research Professor of Demography at Georgetown University, Washington DC.

Professor Feshbach is a former president of the American Association for the Advancement of Slavic Studies and of the Association for Comparative Economic Studies. He is the author of over 100 publications on the demography, economy, and society of the former Soviet Union; his most recent book, with Alfred Friendly Jnr, is Ecocide in the USSR: health and nature under siege *(Aurum Press London, 1992).*

If measured by the dynamics of average life expectancy at birth, then the term 'crisis' applies in full force to the situation of the population of the former Soviet Union (FSU). I do not refer to the lethal use of force that is occurring in areas such as Armenia, Azerbaijan, Georgia and Tadjikistan, but rather to the impact of environmental and health conditions on the populations of the region. Life expectancy has continued to decline since 1989 to an astonishingly low level among men and women of the Russian Federation, the Ukraine, and certainly in the regions of conflict, as well as elsewhere. Internal projections made by a senior demographer for the Russian Federation Council of Ministers projects even further decline—to

---

[1] This chapter is largely based on information in the two state reports on environment for the Russian Federation issued in 1992 and 1993 (*Gosudarstvenny doklad o sostoyanii okruzhayushchey prirodnoy sredy Rossiyskoy Federatsii v 1991 godu* and . . . *v 1992 godu*, and the state report on health issued in 1992 (*Gosudarstvenny doklad o sostoyanii zdorov'ya Rossiyskov Federatsii v 1991 godu*). Other references are listed at the end of the chapter.

below 59 for males in many areas at the turn of the century, 6–7 years hence.

Why? Is this pure 'doom and gloom'? Are the figures cited by the press and sources inside the FSU exaggerated in order to get money from Western governments, banks, charities, individuals? Or are they largely, as I believe, even understated?

Let me begin with two quotes, one a bit older, one made last year (1992) at a press conference announcing the first annual publications on the status of the environment and of the health condition of the population of the Russian Federation.

The earlier statement was made by Dr A. I. Potapov, a former Minister of Health of the RSFSR, who said, (and I quote) 'To live longer, breathe less!' Not very helpful but very indicative. A real example: when speaking at a meeting last year in Odense, Denmark on environmental conditions in the FSU, I cited the case of Nizhniy Tagil, an old metallurgical centre located in the Urals. It is similar to Magnitogorsk, still using very old technology and with inadequate, pollution-abatement equipment (if indeed it can be said to have any). Because the old oxygen-based furnaces need 'fresh' oxygen for their operation, and because the plants have polluted the city so much, a pipeline has been built 3 km outside the city limits to bring in the fresh oxygen required. When I stated this at the Odense conference, the First Deputy Minister of the Environment of Russia, Andrey Poryadin, was quick to point out that the pipeline is now 6 km, not 3, from the city limits. Will it be 9 km next year; 12 km the year after? Will Western assistance be sufficient to the purpose and come in time to save lives? Will we assist, as the Finns and Norwegians are doing at Nikel' in their mutual border regions on the Kola Peninsula, in order to prevent trans-border pollution? Why should these countries not bomb the plant—as the Norwegian Greens have proposed—in order to avoid the consequences of the dangerous pollutants that it emits? Workers in this, the third most profitable plant in all of the Russian Federation, live a mere 34 years on average. Why do they work there? Why do they not leave? Are there alternative places of employment? Will their families who do not work at the plant survive? Considering that average life expectancy for all persons in the city is 44 years, no one can be expected to survive very long. As recently as 3 or 4 years ago, discussion of such questions, let alone revelations, did not occur in public, and perhaps did not even take place in private among employees of the Ministry of Health, statistical authorities, and the Ministry of Environment. The latter did not even exist (its early incarnation was Goskompriroda, the State Committee for Environment) until 1988.

Examples of poor conditions also abound in other locations: Noril'sk, Kemerovo, Dnepropetrovsk, Mariupol', and many, many others; 13 cities were listed in the trade union newspaper, *Trud*, as places where *ne stoit yezdit' na ulitsu* (where it was not worth going out on to the streets) due to pollution. In 1991, in Russia alone, benzo(a)pyrene, a known carcinogen, was found in 160 of the 350 cities monitored, 92 of which were at hazardous levels, potentially increasing the level of cancer among the population. During a drive between Dnepropetrovsk and Mariupol', the former Minister of Environment of the Ukraine, Dr Yuri Shcherbak, told two American senators that they were driving through the 'valley of death'. These conditions have been caused not only by industrial pollution, but also by newly revealed and astonishing levels of radioactivity, chemicals, heavy metals, and toxic waste, by poor-quality food, inadequate nutrition for most, growing drug problems, poor reproductive health of women, and much else.

The second quotation mentioned earlier deals with the very last item cited, that of the reproductive health of women. At the press conference on 7 October 1992, one day after the publication of the two reports, the President of the Russian Academy of Medical Sciences, Dr Pokrovskiy, stipulated that 'Russia is doomed for the next 25 years!' What could this hyperbolic statement mean?

It means, or rather represents, the summation of a large array of facts, trends, and potential problems for the population, some long-term but previously unpublicized, others of recent origin, that have developed in the past 5-10 years.

In the Russian Federation 75 per cent of women have medical problems during their pregnancy including late toxaemia, heart problems, sepsis, anaemia, and other potential dangers to the woman and to the fetus. Only 40 per cent of all children are born healthy. Several years ago, it was reported that even in the Kremlin hospital for the élite only 18 per cent of all children were born without signs of poor health. Moreover, in the State Report on the Health Status of the Population of the Russian Federation, it is recorded that 25 per cent of all children have anaemia, rickets, or hypotrophy during their first 5 years of life. In the United States rickets is no longer recorded because the addition of vitamin D to milk prevents its occurrence. In a report on the growth of infant mortality in the Soviet Union, Davis and Feshbach (1980) noted that rickets leads frequently to pneumonia, and that this contributed to some 25 per cent of all deaths of infants in the then RSFSR. Furthermore, the former Soviet Union is finally adopting—not just in the Russian Federation—the World Health Organization's definition of and

methodology for determining infant mortality. The former definition used by the Soviet Union was so limited that no other country
used it, not even eastern European countries under its control.
According to that definition, if a child born weighing less than
1000 g, of less than 35 cm in length, and of less than 28 weeks' gesta-
tion, died before it was 7 days old, it was counted as a still birth
and not a live birth. The current WHO definition incorporates all
live births of babies weighing 500 g, with no criteria of length of life
and body length. If all statistical reporting agencies of the Russian
Federation conform to this international definition, it is estimated
by Russian demographers and statisticians that, for this reason
alone, the infant mortality rate in Russia will increase by between
25 and 33 per cent. Thus, the current reported rate of some 19.9 per
1000 live births in 1993 will increase to between 25 and 27 per 1000
live births (WHO definition). I would add that if errors of omission
in situations where births are not recorded (perhaps, for example,
because the child dies before registration and the parents reside in
an isolated region of Siberia) and errors of commission, (for example
where the child is not recorded as dying until the thirteenth month)
were also accounted for them the death rate would be even higher.
In Russia, this latter factor alone accounts for a mortality rate
of 19 per cent according to an official survey, *ca.* 1990, and an
estimated rate of 86 per cent in Turkmenistan (survey conducted by
Ye. Andreyev of the Soviet Statistical Agency's Research Institute).
Regrettably, if someone proposed to me that the 'truer' infant
mortality rate in Turkmenistan was between 150 and 200 per 1000
live births, not the 50 or so officially reported, I would be disinclined
to argue.

Infant mortality is high, but so too is mortality among adults.
Thirty per cent of all deaths in 1993 occurred among the working-age
population. Almost one-half of all male deaths occur in the 16 to
59 year age bracket. Children as well as adults are dying at much
higher rates than in previous years from infectious diseases, including the so-called childhood diseases. The most virulent disease of all
is diphtheria, in terms of its increase and impact on the population
over the past 5 years. In St. Petersburg there was a 160-fold increase
in the disease between 1989 and 1992; in Moscow it has increased
from 46 cases recorded in 1988 to perhaps 4000 plus in 1993
(extrapolating from early reports). In the Ukraine, a tenfold increase
in diphtheria cases was recorded in 1 year, between 1990 and 1991.
If one were to extrapolate from the Moscow city rate of diphtheria
to the United States, by applying the rate in the city per 100 000
population, then, instead of 4 cases reported in the entire United

States in 1992, there would have been over 56 000 cases. If the doubling in Russia and Moscow city were to continue apace for 1993, then the extrapolated number in the United States would yield over 100 000 cases in that year. This level would be more than twice the number of cases reported in the United Kingdom in 1940 (albeit with a smaller population), long before there was a diphtheria vaccine.

Immunization coverage is extraordinarily low throughout all of the former Soviet Union. Several years ago, only 70 per cent of the population of Russia had been inoculated against diphtheria, whooping cough, and tetanus, and only 40 per cent of Uzbekistanis. Currently, the Deputy Chief of the State Sanitary–Epidemiological Commission, Anatoliy Monisov, indicates that only 15 per cent of adults have had a full series of vaccinations. Hopefully the recently announced effort to have 90 per cent of children and 70 per cent of adults inoculated by 1995 will be successful, but I doubt that this is possible. There is a shortage of vaccines that the population will trust to be effective and single-use syringes and needles are reused regularly.

There is a desperate lack of vital medicines. Domestically produced insulin, for example, has not been available for purchase by the population since 1990; foreign imports were almost non-existent in 1992. Foreign donations are fine up to a point; beyond that, the need for internal production is necessary. Given the disagreements between the current Minister of Health and many commentators from the pharmaceutical system, this will not be resolved in the short run. Combined with the disarray overall in the economy and society for the immediate future, this bodes ill for any significant resolution of this issue for the moment.

There is no time or space to discuss remarkable increases in tuberculosis, typhoid, measles, mumps, hepatitis, cholera, human anthrax, dysentery, salmonella infections, plague, poliomyelitis, and rubella. The last-mentioned, however, deserves special comment here. Rubella inoculations for new-borns are not even on the immunization calendar in the FSU. During the period 1985–89, the annual average number of cases of rubella recorded in the United States (with some 240–250 million population) was 427 per year; the former Soviet Union (with some 280–285 million population) recorded 564 000 per year.

The potential exists for an explosion of AIDS in the former Soviet Union. Official figures of 50 full-blown AIDS cases, or 500 HIV cases are totally inaccurate. The head of the Central Bureau of Epidemiology, Dr V. V. Pokrovskiy, the son of the President of the Academy of Medical sciences cited earlier, indicated in 1992 that

3000–5000 HIV cases would be more correct. While I believe that the number of HIV cases is much higher, let this suffice for the moment to indicate that official figures and reality are still very disparate. The conditions that will inevitably favour the rapid spread of AIDS are the multiple use of inadequately sterilized syringes, the enormous growth of hard drug abuse, the rise in prostitution, especially child prostitution including girls aged 10 and over, and perhaps the existence of a larger risk population of homosexuals than previously estimated. In a medical institution at Elista in Kalmykia (southern Russia) a nurse used the same (now known to be tainted) syringe and needle, without sterilization between usage, for 24 children who became infected with HIV and then developed AIDS. Registered drug addicts in Moscow City were reported by the Ministry of Internal Affairs (MVD) to number 2000 in 1993; the MVD simultaneously reported that the true number was believed to be between 60 000 and 80 000. Child prostitution, especially with foreign currency clientele, has also led to a statistically significant increase in sexually transmitted diseases. Again, while any comparison is invidious, the FSU is far behind the regrettable lead that the United States maintains on an absolute and relative basis. But the potential for unguarded sexual relations appears to be very high, and concomitantly for a large increase in HIV and thence AIDS. Details on child prostitution among young females are just astonishing. One can be certain, as I am after discussing this with many leading medical and public health officials in Moscow, that there is either no allocation, or totally insufficient resource allocation, for prevention and treatment of AIDS-related diseases in the budgets at any level and in any country of the former Soviet Union.

For these reasons and others, it is difficult to project the population growth of the former Soviet Union in its constituent republics, now countries. Thus, on the one hand, given high fertility one would expect that the republics and countries of Central Asia and Kazakhstan would have high rates of population growth. Total fertility rates (TFRs) have been declining in recent years, but they remain much higher than those of the Slavic countries and certainly much above those of the Baltic region. With four or more children per woman between the ages of 15 and 49 in Kyrgyzstan, Tadjikistan, Turkmenistan and Uzbekistan, as well as among Kazakhs, growth is fully predictable. But the uncertainty of the civil war conditions in Tadjikistan, the occasional fighting over water rights between several of the countries in the region, and continuing very high infant mortality rates continue to affect growth patterns. Clearly, therefore, projections of rates of growth are hazardous, but growth will probably continue at 2 per cent per year or more, especially in Turkmenistan and even in Tadjikistan, given the latter's very high TFRs.

Affecting this region in the southern tier, as well as those countries of other regions, is net migration — net out-migration in the south, net in-migration in the Slavic countries of Russia, Belorussia, and the Ukraine, and net out-migration in the Baltic countries of Estonia, Latvia, and Lithuania. In the Baltic countries the out-migration of the Russian military should be completed in 1994. Given relatively low crude birth rates and relatively high crude death rates (because of the age structure of the population), we can expect a short-term low rate of growth, and something of an increase thereafter. In Russia the situation is more complicated. Large numbers of refugees, combined with migrants, have added some several millions to the population in recent years. This trend will decrease in the future, but will continue to have a large potential since more than 20 million ethnic Russians reside in the 'near abroad' — the countries of the former Soviet Union excluding the Russian Federation itself. Moreover, the levels may accelerate if ethnic conflicts, citizenship and language laws reflecting local nationalism add to the problems in these other countries.

Simultaneously, in 1992 two of every three conceptions were aborted, the number of births being recorded as one-half the number of abortions recorded. If illegal abortions (that is, those performed outside of medical institutions) are also counted, then the share of live births is even less. Economic, social, and political concerns add to the uncertainty of family planning decisions. Thus, the overall projection is for a continuing reduction in the absolute size of the populations of the Russian Federation. Thus far the Russian Federation has avoided patterns of conflict which have arisen in Armenia, Azerbaijan, Georgia, and Tadjikistan, but any large-scale civil war within the Russian Federation would add to further reductions in population size. Current internal projections made for the Russian Council of Minsters anticipate a decline of between 2 and 4 million persons by the end of the century.

Belorussian and Ukrainian prospects are clouded by the potential long-term effects of the Chernobyl accident as well as by economic disarray, especially in the Ukraine. If we add the Transcaucasus, with its civil wars in Georgia and the large-scale fighting between Armenia and Azerbaijan, it would be foolhardy to make firm projections. Stagnation in numbers or perhaps some decline can be anticipated net of any migration of refugees from other combat zones or from other areas, such as was caused by the recent eviction of 'illegals' and others from Moscow. In sum, the total population for the entire territory of the former Soviet Union will probably be lower rather than higher, and much less than Western estimates hitherto, and this is before we have even fully considered the environmental impact on health and population patterns.

The poor reproductive health of women which was referred to earlier is also likely to be associated with the impact of the environment. There has been a significant increase in congenital anomalies, from 12.9 per 1000 births in 1986 to 18.7 in 1991 in the USSR, an increase of almost 45 per cent in only 5 years. For this and many other reasons, including radioactivity and chemical hazards, I fear for the gene pool of the entire former Soviet Union. On this sad and perhaps hyperbolic note, I now turn to more specifically environmental issues.

In view of new information, it is clear that *Ecocide in the USSR* (Feshbach and Friendly 1992) understates the range and depth of the health and environmental problems of the former Soviet Union. As noted already, life expectancy continues to decline; mortality increases; health services, especially medicines, are less available; and child health is worse. Moreover, radioactivity, poor water quality, atmospheric pollution, chemicals, heavy metals, land erosion, and other factors are officially — let alone unofficially — reported to be a greater danger than was revealed previously.

New information about levels of radioactivity, about the spread of chemicals in the air, land, and water, including chemical weapons and liquid rocket fuel (heptyl, a supertoxic chemical compound), about the spread of heavy metals and mineral salts throughout the region, all attest to the ecological and health situation being worse than heretofore reported. Yablokov asserted that up to 35 per cent of the population residing in industrial regions suffers from immunodeficiencies (Yablokov 1992). While it is not clear what he is including, or how it is measured, the assertion itself is clearly disturbing if even half true. The lower priority accorded by the government to resource allocation to the environment compared with production will add to pollution and health hazards.

The transition in the former Soviet Union to the efficient use of available energy resources is still far too low. The nuclear industry continues, albeit at a lower level than projected earlier. Moreover, the nuclear lobby has obtained government approval for the industry to grow, arguing that oil supplies will dwindle until Western investment fully operates and economic returns become available to the Western investor. In addition, there are derivative benefits for the military from continued operations in the nuclear sector. Furthermore, natural gas production currently does not satisfy demand, and the available coal seams are of high sulphur content. The major consequence is dependency on nuclear energy. Despite all past problems in operating, maintaining, and securing nuclear power plants, plans have been adopted for the share of nuclear energy in the fuel and energy balance almost to double by the year 2010. The quality of operating personnel, with their demands for more pay as well as better operating conditions during a long-term period of fiscal constraint, leads to questions of nuclear security, reflected in the apprehension of Western as well as Russian commentators about safety and the potential theft of nuclear materials.

Aleksey Yablokov, Presidential Advisor for Environment and Health in Russia, has forcefully denounced the expansion plans for the nuclear power industry (see, for instance, Escalona (1994), Shumova (1993)). He seeks alternative sources of energy production in new, energy-efficient gas turbines. Moreover, he is very concerned, as are others, with the human factor in atomic power plant operations. According to his estimates, human error accounts for 75 per cent of the underlying causes of accidents at these facilities. Considered by Yablokov to be the area of highest priority for environmental and health security, radioactivity-linked pollution is much more widespread and dangerous than previously realized. Information is coming to light on a wide range of issues that could potentially lead to serious environmental and health catastrophes. These include:

- new evaluations of the spread and depth of radioactivity emanating from the Chernobyl accident and of the health impact of the accident;
- new reports on nuclear waste dumping in the waters to the north and east of the former Soviet Union;
- new information about the danger and extent of stocks of liquid rocket fuel;
- new information about the numbers and location of nuclear-powered submarines awaiting dismantling;
- new information about the extent of the 'secret city' network of the nuclear and chemical sectors of the military–industrial complex;
- new information about the lack of security at nuclear facilities, leading to concerns about theft of nuclear materials, smuggling, and therefore potential use by terrorists;
- new concerns about poor attentiveness to operations of facilities using radioactive materials, leading to such accidents as occurred in April 1993 at Tomsk-7 and July 1993 at Chelyabinsk-65.

Pokrovskiy's statement, cited earlier, about the negative prospects for Russia in the next quarter of a century, whether viewed as hyperbole, self-interest, or scientific judgement, underscores the interaction and interrelationship of ecological and health issues. Concerns about the gene pool of the country and about growth in morbidity and mortality, have clearly led to his and others' predictions of a negative future for the population of Russia. Similar remarks have been made by Ukrainian, Belorussian, and Kazakh medical personnel, legislators, and other commentators. The key concern for the Ukraine and Belorussia is the fallout from nuclear accidents or the accidental release of radioactivity impacting on their territory.

In early 1992, the Belarus Minister of Health invited the Regional Office for Europe of the World Health Organization (WHO) to select a team of health specialists to verify new findings about a major incidence of thyroid cancer. According to the review of 104 histological slides of papillary carcinoma cells conducted by Dr Keith Baverstock and his team, it was found that 102 had been correctly diagnosed. Past claims were thought to have been exaggerated in order to obtain funding, or to have been the result of poor diagnostics by Soviet physicians in the post-Chernobyl explosion period. Until this WHO examination of the health impact of Chernobyl, very little credence had been given to the alleged dimension of the medical problem. Based on this examination, Baverstock reported that the thyroid cancer rate was 80 per million persons, not 1 per million, and that the cancer is very aggressive (Baverstock 1993). Consequently, in the near term (7–10 years after the 1986 accident) we can expect many more cases in the regions with contamination from Chernobyl, especially among children. These findings directly contradict the International Atomic Energy Agency's report of 1989 that there was and would be very little health impact from the release of radioactive materials into the atmosphere at Chernobyl. In addition there is uneasiness about the $1000 \, m^2$ ($11\,000 \, ft^2$) of cracks and openings in the sarcophagus of block number 4 at Chernobyl. (Large numbers of cracks are now being found by the representatives of the Swedish Radiation Institute in the Ignalina nuclear power plant structure itself.) Yuri Shcherbak, the former Ukrainian minister of Environment, and other leading observers in Ukraine indicate that release of additional radioactivity could penetrate the water aquifer of Kiev and the atmosphere. Construction of a new sarcophagus around the old, hastily built sarcophagus may be inappropriate if the weight of this new encasement leads to additional danger; some environmentalists in the former Soviet Union worry that the weight of a new concrete structure could lead to a shift in the subsurface land. This would cause the roof to fall from its precarious position on the edge of one of the walls in the now 'contained' structure. One result would be the release of significant quantities of radioactive dust and of still-present unburned radioactive fuel into the atmosphere.

Much evidence exists of past and present dumping of radioactive toxic waste into the northern and far-eastern waters, only partly because of lack of burial grounds on land. In addition, pollution caused by PCBs (polychlorinated biphenols) and DDT, by petroleum products, and, in some areas, by nuclear reactors dumped with live reactors and rods is also reported. Very probably there are other contaminants in the water, on land, and in the air that remain undisclosed — particularly in the 'secret cities' of the military's nuclear, chemical, and bacteriological warfare sector.

Early in 1993, the location and amount of radioactive toxic waste dumping was revealed. According to the Yablokov Commission's report (1993), the dumping took place in the Barents and Kara seas of the Arctic region, and the Sea of Okhotsk and other areas in the Sea of Japan near Korea and Japan (Yablokov 1993). If we count chemical weapons among chemical pollutants requiring significant clean-up, then the latest revelations about not only the dumping of 30 000 to 40 000 tonnes of Second World War chemical weapons into the Baltic Sea, as 'revealed previously', but also of 400 000 tonnes or more of various hazardous substances are stunning. The problem may be mitigated if the materials and their containers leak slowly and are exposed to the seas' hydrolysing process. But if they leak rapidly a major environmental health hazard may be created for the populations of the Baltic Sea region.

As in the case of chemical weapons dumped into Baltic Sea, the plutonium-tipped torpedoes of the nuclear submarine *Komsomolets* (which is now located at the bottom of the sea off the coast of Norway) are also subject to corrosion. If they leak slowly rather than quickly, the release of toxic materials will not be very dangerous. If quick release occurs, the health of adjacent populations may be endangered through the food chain.

Nuclear waste storage sites and reprocessing facilities are the focus of a major new 200 billion rouble programme adopted in the spring of 1993 by the Ministry of Atomic Industry. A principal site for the clean-up operations under this programme is Mayak (alternatively called Chelyabinsk-40, later Chelyabinsk-65) where radiation from an accident in 1957, an accident in 1967 at Lake Karachay from dumping, and uncontained dumping of radioactive waste beginning in earlier years into the Techa River, is recorded even now at 600 roentgens/hour (155 mC/kg/h); normal background radiation is approximately 10–12 microroentgens/hour (2.6–3.1 nc/kg/h).

Programme activities also include an assessment of the radioactivity present at sites 600 to 2800 m below ground at the 79 locations in the Russian Federation where underground and nuclear explosions took place after 1963 'for peaceful purposes'. Rehabilitation is necessary, and is authorized by the new programme. Given that we now know that between 115 and 120 'civilian' nuclear explosions were conducted throughout the former Soviet Union, then there are at least 36 other sites in Kazakhstan and the Ukraine that should also be examined for residual radioactivity. For example, radioactivity has been found in some oil fields in Kazakhstan as well as in the diamond fields of Yakutiya (Sakha Republic) of the Russian Federation. Radioactivity will probably be found elsewhere and future Western investment must be cognizant of this fact in making assessments of costs associated with the development of such locales.

Plans for disarmament and dismantlement of nuclear submarines in the Shkotovo region have heightened Japanese concern. Greenpeace's Joshua Handler has documented an accident in August 1985 at the Shkotovo-22 site (Handler 1993, 1994). Radioactivity was released when a reactor was being replaced. Fear of similar 'accidents' combined with the recent release of the Yablokov report on nuclear waste dumping in the region has impelled the Japanese government to follow these activities attentively. The Scandinavian countries are also attentive to and worried about these operations. The recent reclosing of Severodvinsk as a forbidden zone may contribute further to outside worries about the environmental and health hazards during the process of disarmament of intercontinental ballistic missiles, and decommissioning of nuclear submarines. How the Russian government and its military authorities expect assistance to be forthcoming to help pay for disarmament if they re-establish a zone of no access is unclear.

Russian environmentalists and officials fear the unknown situation in the secret network of cities in the nuclear and chemical sectors and this adds to the difficulty of reducing environmental threats. The potential for accidents in locations that are not normally open to non-military personnel may be either greater or lower than can be guessed at, but secrecy itself contributes to uncertainty. It was only in May of 1992 (after *Ecocide in the USSR* was published) that the first serious discussion of secret cities occurred, and that was outside the country. Viktor Mikhailov, the Minister of the Atomic Industry, spoke at a meeting in Stavanger, Norway, about this network (Felgengaller 1992); very little had appeared in the media prior to that. It was a rare event for any Western observer to go to one of these cities.

Urban land is also highly polluted. Evidence now available shows not only radioactive but also heavy metal toxic waste sites and 'normal' toxic industrial waste abundantly spread throughout the urban scene. The full extent of chemical-related pollution of land, air, water is not known, but, as with radioactivity, it appears to be much more complex and widespread, and therefore more of a danger to health, than had previously been suggested. The chemical compound dioxin is so widespread on the land — as well as in air and water — that the country may be at a much greater hazard level from this than from any other cause. Dioxin is produced directly or as a by-product in various sectors of the economy. In the autumn of 1992, for the first time, details of the total quantity of anthropogenic emissions of dioxin in Russia were published by the now former head of the Hydrometeorological Service, Dr Yuri Izrael' (Izrael' *et al.* 1992). To the extent that this 'production' gets into the ambient air, land, and water, it contributes significantly to the environmental problems of the country.

Pollution from chemical plants, in particular in cities in which the chemical industry is associated with production for the defence sector, is consistently at levels that have a major influence on the health of the resident populations. Atmospheric pollution, according to the State Report on Environment (1991), is estimated to be responsible (causal) for 20 to 30 per cent of the overall illness of the population. Ferrous metallurgy in Magnitogorsk, Novokuznetsk, Nizhniy Tagil, Lipetsk, and other cities is blamed in the 1992 Environmental Status report for illness rates among children and adults which are approximately 40 per cent higher than in relatively clean cities. According to Fedorov, a dissident chemist formerly employed by the chemical weapons industry, dioxin is not discussed because much of it emanates from secret military facilities of the Khimprom (chemical industry) network (Fedorov 1992). Such facilities exist in 29 cities of the former Soviet Union. Dioxin, mentioned as one of the by-products of incomplete combustion of fossil fuels, is also a potential pollutant from its use in agriculture, and is also produced when organic compounds dumped or released into bodies of water are combined with chlorine. A letter written by the heads of the KGB, Gosplan (the State Planning Committee), and the Academy of Sciences of the USSR to then President Gorbachev, in response to his Presidential Directive No. 74355, dated 21 December 1990, stipulated that dioxin was a greater threat to the Soviet Union than any other environmental factor (presumably excluding nuclear war). They also stipulated that despite its toxicity, dioxin had not been the subject of appropriate attention until that point in time. The lack of attention to all toxic materials has led to 'a result in which the unsatisfactory impact of chemical and other negative factors on the health status of the populations calls for deep anxiety'. Environmental degradation underlies many of the serious health problems of the population of the former Soviet Union (Feshbach 1995).

From 1945 to 1967 leftover chemical weapons were dumped into the North Sea and Baltic by the British, and into the Baltic Sea by the American and the Soviet governments. The Soviets also dumped poison gas into the Sea of Japan. Now, almost 50 years after the initial period of this dumping activity, many Russian and Baltic, as well as Western analysts, are apprehensive about the danger to the states bordering the Baltic Sea; others are less apprehensive because they expect the chemical release to be diluted by the wave action of the sea.

Outside the four countries of Scandinavia (Denmark, Norway, Sweden, and Finland), the three Baltic countries (Estonia, Latvia, and Lithuania), and the remaining three members of the Baltic Sea Convention (Poland, Germany, and Russia), very little attention is paid to the contamination of the entire Baltic region with chemical weapons. Yet the danger may be very great to the populations of these countries and perhaps beyond. Although known and discussed previously in various sources, the impact on the consciousness of the world seems to have been minimal. Discussions at Geneva by the United Nations did not result in any major effort to mitigate the potential hazards of these chemical-weapon dumpings.

Alleged production of unique, hazardous chemicals for use in military weapons is the subject of much controversy. The revelations of two scientists, Drs Vil Miryazanov and Lev Fedorov, have brought the issue of treaty compliance as well as environmental hazards to a new level. Miryazanov and Fedorov have been subjected to investigation and prosecution for disclosing secret information. Reports abound that there was secret production of chemicals for use in binary bombs, and extremely toxic chemical warfare developments; if these reports are true, this could well turn out to be a threat to the global environment.

Seven nuclear blasts reportedly conducted in the region of Kemerovo (Western Siberia) were intended, in part, to open pits for dumping of toxic waste created by the city. Readings of 160 microroentgens/hour (40 nc/kg/h) at the site of the cavity are more than 10 times the normal background radiation. Given the admixture of chemical and other pollutants, it is hard to single out a particular cause for the increase in birth defects and deformities reported in Kemerovo and elsewhere, but chemicals undoubtedly play a very large part in the accumulating trend in poorer health of the populations throughout the region.

Information about the large quantity and the hazardous quality of the principal liquid rocket fuel produced in the former Soviet Union is worrisome to say the least. Heptyl is clearly the 'prime hazard' liquid rocket fuel which caused the contamination of more than 8 million hectares in the Plesetsk test range area in the Arkhangel'sk region, described by Vladimir Karasev, Responsible Secretary of the Ecological Policy Council in the office of the President of the Russian Federation (Karasev 1993). Spills and parts of booster rockets jettisoned over regions of difficult access add to the problem of detoxifying soil and bodies of water in these locales.

Japanese officials are so concerned about the potential danger from this fuel — especially in the Sea of Japan region — that they have requested permission from the Russian government to send in teams of technicians and advisors to help reduce the danger. In the Baltic region, abandonment of a missile site by the Russian military led to the discovery that '270 tons of highly toxic rocket fuel' are stored at the site. Fearing possible health problems, the local government refused to assume control for the camp, leaving the area unguarded and posing a clear hazard to the population's health and environment of the area near Ventspils. Will this be repeated at other abandoned missile sites? Will potential terrorists get access to the materials? Are national or local governments aware of the toxicity of this and other similar sites?

Details made available in 1992 on the extent of wind and water erosion, salination, swamping, waterlogging, compacting of the earth, and loss of humus demonstrate that land-use problems abound throughout the FSU (Moscow 1991). Some 50 per cent of all arable land needs remediation, improvement, and better management. Significant increases in agricultural productivity will depend upon both the removal of these environmental constraints, and the privatization of the farming sector.

Desertification in Kalmykia in Russia and in the Aral Sea region of Central Asia contributes to surprising decreases in the amount of available arable land. The desiccation of the Aral Sea is leading to the formation of another desert in a region already containing a desert (Kyzyl-kum). Environmental hazards emanate from salt and dust storms. Between 15 and 75 million tonnes of salt and dust are lifted every year into the air from the Aral basin. They are carried as far as 500 miles (800 km) from the former Aral Sea region.

Sustainable land-use projects are urgently needed, as is better water management. Economic stresses on the land from poor management directly affect forest survival, and swamping leads to diminution in the productivity of land.

In the draft report prepared by Goskompriroda to the Rio Summit, many details which underscore the depth of the problem were published for the entire territory. Of the 600.1 million hectares used for agriculture in the former Soviet Union (equivalent to 6 million km^2 — 11 times larger than the area of France, 70 times larger than Austria), about 500 million hectares is arable land, of which some 225 million hectares were under cultivation in 1990 (Golitsyn 1993). About 97 million hectares of all agricultural land in 1990 was salinated, of which 19 million hectares were arable land; 68 million hectares were acidified, of which 16 million were arable land. Chemical pollution of the air has reduced the forest area, according to official estimates for the past 2 decades, by almost 600 000 hectares, and threatens an additional 1 million hectares.

In the State Report on Environment issued on 6 October 1992, the Sysin Scientific Research Institute on Man and Hygiene of the Environment of the Russian Academy of Medical Sciences is cited as the source for the finding that only 15 per cent of the urban population of Russia lives in 'ecologically acceptable levels of pollution'. Obversely, 85 per cent do not live in healthy places. At first glance these ratios may not seem possible because air pollution reportedly had decreased during the period 1989–91. The total amount of pollutants emitted by industry into the atmosphere was 35.5 million tonnes in 1989, 34.3 million tonnes in 1990, and 31.8 million tonnes in 1991. However, looking behind these numbers, which appear to show a drop in air pollution emissions, we find that the amount recorded was affected by non-production (and concomitant non-emission of pollution) during the many strikes at industrial plants during this period, by the shortage of fuels which prevented them from operating, and by the disarray in the agencies responsible for these measurements.

The atmosphere needs protection not only through better environmental pollution control devices but also through energy substitutions of less hazardous fuels for energy production, as well as new energy-efficient equipment such as gas turbines. Benzo[a]pyrene (BP) is among the worst and most widespread of pollutants that clearly affect the health of the population. By 1991, the prevalence of BP was much greater than in 1989. At the earlier date, BP was recorded in 67 Soviet cities at five times or more the maximum pollution concentration allowed by the regulations of the Ministry of

Health and the Ministry of Environment. By 1991, in Russia alone, of 350 cities monitored by the Russian Ministry of Environment, BP was recorded in 160 cities, of which 92 were found to be at a hazardous level. A carcinogenic by-product of the combustion of coal at thermal power plants, BP is probably a major cause of high rates of malignant tumours found in many cities.

Toxic chemicals are rarely safely used in the former Soviet Union. 'Pesticidal Chernobyl' is the hyperbolic but pointed title of an article written in the leading national medical newspaper about the Kuban Region (Aleksayeva 1992). In Krasnodarsk Kray, the use of pesticides is, on average, five times higher than the average for all of the Russian Federation. A cancer rate six times higher than the average incidence rate of cancer for Russia as a whole is attributed to the heavy usage of pesticides. The anthropogenic hazard of these pesticides is such that it has led Aleksayeva to assert that some regions will not have any healthy children at all in 10–15 years (Aleksayeva 1992). Excessive loads of herbicides and chemical fertilizers undoubtedly continue. Even though the use of DDT was prohibited by international agreement in 1970–72 by almost all countries, including the former Soviet Union, farms employed it, often to excess, until very recently.

Industrial accidents contribute very significantly to pollution of the land near industrial sites, as do railroad transportation accidents and breaks in pipelines throughout the entire region. Two major oil and gas pipeline spills occur every day every year; 10 per cent of these pipelines have been in use for over 35 years. According to the Russian Academy of Sciences, 10 years is considered to be the operational life of such pipelines, and this maximal level also is considered excessive and leads to an unreliable transport system. Some 28 000 ruptures in the pipelines were recorded in 1991 alone. This number must add significantly to the total population at hazard.

Costly accidents, disasters, and other occurrences involve a loss of over 1 billion roubles every 10–15 years. Accidents and disasters involving losses from 200 million up to 1 billion roubles (prices as of early 1993) occur once every 8–12 months, and those involving losses up to 200 million roubles, every 15–45 days. Even considering current inflation patterns, these numbers begin to add up to 'real money'. Hopefully the attention being paid to this issue, including better reporting, will serve to reduce these unfortunate events. Given the current drive to produce more goods regardless of the environment, it is likely that accidents will continue to plague the economy, the environment, and the health of populations exposed to these events.

Three-quarters of all surface water is polluted, and even after treatment only half is drinkable. What is even more clear now is the dimension of the chemical danger and the underlying pollutants that are contributing to the degradation of the water. Wastewater treatment equipment and facilities date largely from designs from the 1950s and 1960s and are not capable of handling the demands on them. According to the head of the Laboratory for Purification of Natural Waters of the National Research Institute for Water Geology, the treatment facilities are capable of handling natural mineral pollutants, clays, water algae, but no 'oil, radioactive substances and acids' (Loukjanenko 1990). Consequently, the principal defence against polluted wastewater at present is chlorine which has the potential for causing environmental and health hazards when being transported throughout the region. More than a disinfectant, chlorine becomes a potential danger when combined with organic substances, forming dioxin or other toxic compounds. According to the World Resources Institute, chlorine is effective when added to water to eliminate bacteria and bad odours, but when reacting with dissolved organic matter it will produce carcinogenics such as chloroform and trihalomethanes (World Resources Institute 1993).

Yablokov told a correspondent of *The Financial Times* in the spring of 1993 that 2 years earlier one-quarter of the water supplied in the former USSR to residences and one-third of that supplied to institutions was 'insufficiently cleaned' (Boulton 1993). A direct consequence of this was further increases in the number of digestive illnesses, including cholera. User fees and polluter fines are his recommendations for the future, if they can be enforced and, I would add, if the rates were significant burdens so that they would be efficacious enough to reduce use and pollution. The early years of recording and analysing the content of the water supply may have been incorrect, with deliberate recording at only a low level, and better measuring instruments have become available, but even so there has been an astonishing growth in contamination in the past decade. During the period 1979–90, a geometric increase in incidence of microbes, especially *E. coli* has been recorded in some localities.

Not under the sea, but with a clear and present danger that could threaten the entire Baltic Sea region, is a radioactive toxic waste site in a formerly closed Soviet military city in Estonia. Located only 9 m (30 ft) from the Gulf of Finland, which leads directly into the Baltic Sea, is a toxic waste earthen dam. The dam's embankment is 9 m (30 ft) in width, and 18 m (60 ft) high. This artificial lake is located 90 km (45 miles) east of Tallinn, near the Russian border, and is the holding pond for the nearby Sillimae uranium ore concentration plant. If the dam bursts or has a major leak then, in addition to the contamination of the ground and nearby waters, massive amounts of low- and middle-level radioactive waste will affect the Gulf and then the Baltic Sea.

Writing in 1990 for the World Health Organization, the then head of the Soviet Academy of Sciences' Laboratory of the Institute of Freshwater Biology indicated that the annual average pesticide concentration in the Sea of Azov quintupled in the 5 year period from 1983 to 1987. By 1988, 1 year later, the concentration had increased by 17 times compared with the base year of 1983 (Loukjanenko 1990). Only 10 per cent of the total volume of water in the Black Sea near the surface is oxygenated the anaerobic conditions being largely the result of large-scale industrial pollution. The Danube, the Don, the Dnieper, and the South Bug rivers contribute massive amounts of pollutants. One of the consequences, in economic terms, is the reduction of the annual fish catch by two-thirds in the past 7 years.

One could call this 'crisis upon crisis'. Hopefully these population, health, and environmental crises will be resolved simultaneously with, if not before, the economic and political crises in the former Soviet Union. Otherwise the future appears bleak for the next generation or even beyond.

REFERENCES

Aleksayeva, E. (1992). Pestitsidnyy Chernobyl. *Meditsinskaya Gazeta*, No. 62 (5287), 7 August 1992, p. 11.

Baverstock, K. (1993). Thyroid cancer in children. *World Health Statistics Quarterly*, Vol. 46, No. 3, p. 204.

Boulton, L. (1993). Leyla Bolton samples Russia's contaminated supplies. *Financial Times*, 7 April.

Davis, C. and Feshbach, M. (1980). *Rising infant mortality in the USSR in the 1970s*. International Population Reports, Series P-95, No. 74. US Bureau of Census, Washington, DC.

Escalona, M. C. (1994). Interview with Aleksey Yablokov. *CIS Environmental Watch*, No. 6, Spring 1994, p. 51.

Fedorov, L. (1992). The dioxin expanse of the former USSR: its system of coordinates is built on secrecy, lies and incompetence. *Nezavisimaya Gazeta*, 16 June 1992, p. 6; translated in JPRS, *JPRS Report: Environmental Issues*, JPRS-TEN-92-009, 22 May 1992, p. 68.

Felgengaller, P. (1992). Russia's closed cities. *Nezavisimaya Gazeta*, 30 June 1992, p. 5; translated in JPRS, *JPRS Report: Engineering and Equipment*, JPRS-UEQ-92-011, 6 October 1992, p. 14.

Feshbach, M. (ed.) (1995). *Environmental and health atlas of Russia*. Moscow (in press).

Feshbach, M. and Friendly, A. Jr. (1992). *Ecocide in the USSR: Health and Nature under siege.* Basic Books, New York.

Golitsyn, G. S. (1993). Ecological problems in the CIS during the transitional period. *RFE/RL Research Report,* 22 July.

Handler, J. (1993). Soviet subs—a neglected time bomb. *Christian Science Monitor,* 18 December 1993, p. 19.

Handler, J. (1994). Russia's Pacific fleet—submarine bases and facilities. *Jane's Intelligence Review,* April 1994, p. 166.

Izrael', Y. A. *et al.* (1992). K probleme zagryazneniya prirody sredy benz(a)pirenum. *Meteorologiya i gidrologiya,* 9 September 1992.

Karasev, V. (1993). The defence industry is destroying the natural world, but it can help too. *Rossiyskiye Vesti,* 19 March 1993, p. 3; translated in JPRS, *JPRS Report: Environmental Issues,* JPRS-TEN-93-010, 20 April 1993, p. 23.

Loukjanenko, V. (1990). Water crisis in the USSR. *World Health,* January–February.

Moscow (1991). Ministerstvo prirodopol'zovaniya i okhrany okruzhayushchey sredi SSSR. *Proyekt. Natsional'nyy doklad SSSR k Konferentsii OON 1992 goda po okruzhayushchey srede i razvitiyu.* Moskow.

Shumova, T. (1993). Interview with Aleksey Yablokov, 'My znaem, kak ostanovit' lavinu'. *Svet,* June 1993, p. 6.

State Report on the Environment (1991). Ministerstvo ekologii i prirodnykh resursov Rossiyskoy Federatsii, *Gosudarstvennyy doklad o sostoyanii okruzzhayushchey prirodnoy sredy Rossiyskoy Federatsii v 1991 godu,* p. 36. Moscow.

World Resources Institute (1993). *The 1993 Information Please Environmental Almanac,* p. 36. Houghton Mifflin, Boston.

Yablokov, A. (1993). *Fakty i problemy, svyaz s zakhoroneniyem radioaktivnykh otkhodov v moryakh, omyvayushchikh territoriyu Rossiyskoy Federatsii,* Administration of the President of the Russian Federation, Moscow.

Yavdolyuk, N. (1992). Interview with Aleksey Yablokov by Nadezhda Yavdolyuk, 'the Stalker'. *Moskovskiy Komsomolets,* 5 February 1992, p. 2; translated in JPRS, *JPRS Report: Environmental Issues,* JPRS-TEN-92-008, 5 May 1992, p. 71.

Index